Town of Lincoln Ontario in Colour Photos, Saving Our History One Photo at a Time

Photography
by Barbara Raué
2018

Series Name:
Cruising Ontario

Book 195: Beamsville, Vineland, Jordan, Ball's Falls, Campden

Cover photo: 4225 Fly Road, Campden, Page 65

Series Name: Cruising Ontario
Saving Our History One Photo at a Time
in colour photos

Books Available in Alphabetical Order:
Aberfoyle, Acton, Alton, Amherstburg, Ancaster, Arthur, Aylmer, Ayr, Belleville, Bloomingdale, Brantford, Brockville, Burford, Burlington, Caledon, Caledonia, Cambridge, Clifford, Conestogo, Delhi, Dorchester to Aylmer, Drayton, Drumbo, Dundas, Eden Mills, Elmira, Elora, Erin, Essex, Fergus, Goderich, Guelph, Hagersville, Hamilton, Hanover, Harriston, Hespeler, Jarvis, Kingston, Kingsville, Kitchener, Lake Superior, Linwood, Listowel, London, Lucknow, Merrickville, Mono, Mount Forest, Neustadt, New Hamburg, Newboro, Niagara-on-the-Lake, Oakville, Orangeville, Orillia, Owen Sound, Palmerston, Paris, Perth, Peterborough, Petrolia, Port Colborne, Port Elgin, Portland, Preston, Rockwood, Sarnia, Sault Ste. Marie, Seaforth, Sheffield, Shelburne, Simcoe, Smiths Falls, Southampton, St. George, St. Jacobs, St. Marys, St. Thomas, Stoney Creek, Stratford, Thamesford, Thunder Bay, Tillsonburg, Waterdown, Waterford, Waterloo, Welland, Wellesley, Westport, Windsor, Wingham, Woodstock

Book 184: Mt Pleasant,
    Onondaga, Newport
Book 185-186: Grimsby
Book 187: Toronto
Book 188: Collingwood
Book 189-193: St. Catharines
Book 194: Smithville
Book 195: Town of Lincoln

Table of Contents

Beamsville	Page 5
Vineland	Page 44
Jordan	Page 48
Ball's Falls	Page 59
Campden	Page 63
Town of Lincoln	Page 66
Architectural Terms	Page 67
Building Styles	Page 70

    Clinton Township included the villages of Beamsville, Vineland, Campden and Tintern. Many of the early settlers were Mennonites who emigrated from Pennsylvania.

    Beamsville, Ontario was named after Jacob Beam, a United Empire Loyalist. Jacob and Catharine, along with their daughter Catharine and son-in-law Samuel Merrell, immigrated to Canada from New Jersey in 1788, and founded Beamsville. It was located on the Great Western Railway. In 1898, hockey players in the town of Beamsville were the first to make use of a hockey net.

    In 1970, the Town of Beamsville was amalgamated with Clinton Township and half of Louth Township to form the larger Town of Lincoln. Beamsville is in the heart of Ontario's wine country in the Niagara Peninsula. Many wineries from the area have received top awards, including Grape King at the Niagara Grape & Wine Festival, as well as international awards.

Vineland is bordered by the Twenty Mile Creek and Jordan to the east, Lake Ontario to the north, Beamsville to the west, and Pelham to the south. Vineland is primarily an agricultural community with many fruit farms and wineries. Vineland's fruit crops include cherries, peaches, apples and pears.

Most of the early settlers of Jordan were German in origin, and were devout practicing Mennonites. With a large natural harbor at the mouth of Twenty Creek, Jordan became a busy shipping center for the export of logs for boat masts, tan bark, hides, ashes used in industrial centers for the manufacture of soap, as well as grain, flour, fruit and fruit products. A small ship building industry existed for a time on the banks of the Twenty.

Ball's Falls is a historical ghost town located in the Niagara Region and dates back to the early 19th century when it was established by Jacob Ball, a United Empire Loyalist. After the American Revolution, Jacob and his family were forced from their home and potash works in New York. Twenty Mile Creek, which runs through the area, has two waterfalls. The Ball brothers built a grist mill, a saw mill at the lower falls and a woolen mill at the upper falls. In the late 1850s, the Great Western Railway was established and many industries moved away from here to be closer to the railway. In 1962 Manly Ball sold the land to the Niagara Peninsula Conservation Area and the town, now known as Ball's Falls, is a tourist attraction.

The first settlers of Campden were former members of Butler's Rangers who were granted land for their services to the Crown following the American Revolution. Benjamin Doyle was one of these and he severed part of his land to the newly arrived Pennsylvania Dutch, which included Jacob Moyer and his seven sons. In 1862 when a post office was established, the hamlet was named Campden.

Beamsville

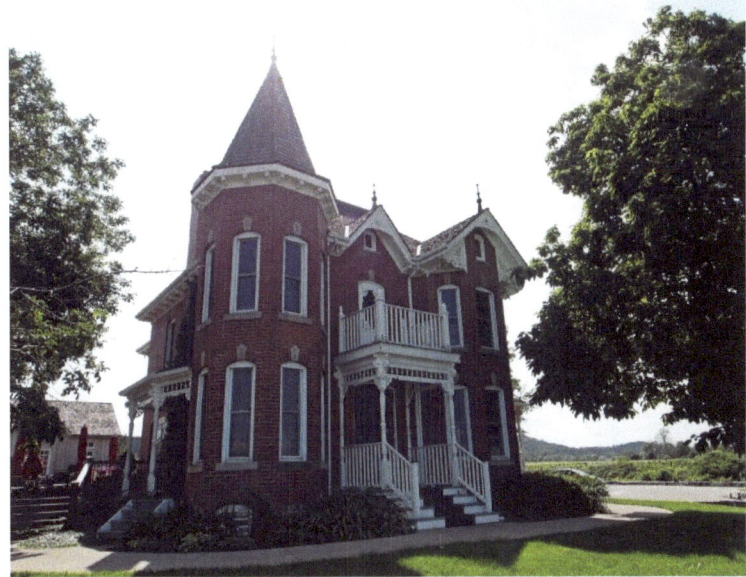

5600 King Street West – The property was a Crown Grant of 52 acres to a loyalist from New Jersey named William W. Kitchen around 1790. He married Alice Beam and together they had nine children. William and Alice's youngest son, Jacob married Jane Dennis. Their only son, William Dennis Kitchen married Margaret Henry and built the house in 1885 on the bench of the escarpment, just west of the Thirty Mile Creek. The house was built in the Queen Anne Revival style with red bricks. The turret has square and rounded cedar shingles, topped with a finial. There are two tall corbeled chimneys, and a hipped roof with a flat belvedere. The gables have carved fretwork brackets and barge board. The tall bay windows are topped with segmental arches and decorative keystones. The front porch has an overhead balcony, and like the side porches, features turned posts, balustrades, spandrels and brackets.

Purchased by the Longwell family in the 1920s, Doug and Jean Longwell continued to live there until the 1980s. From 1999 to 2009, the house was owned and restored by Norman and Sherry Beal, who transformed the property into an estate winery. In 2009 Wendy Midgley and her husband Chef Ross Midgley purchased the Kitchen House and the Coach House from the Beals.

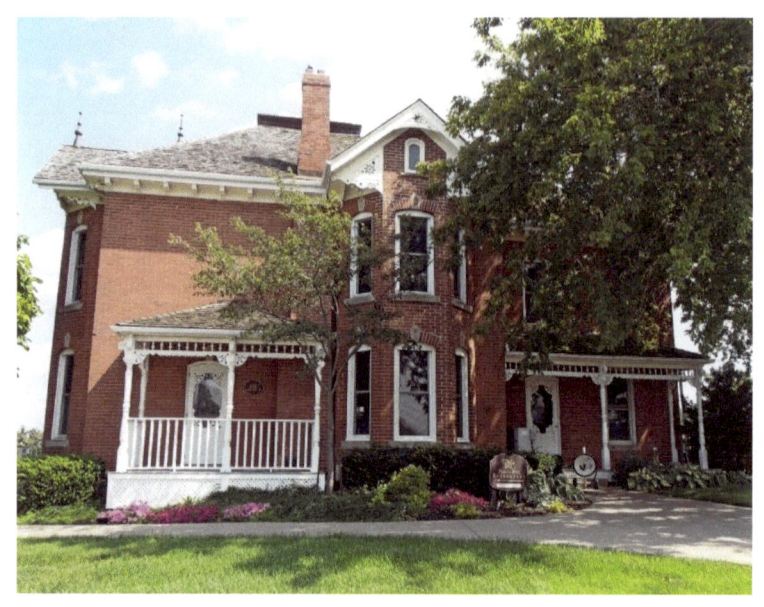

5600 King Street West

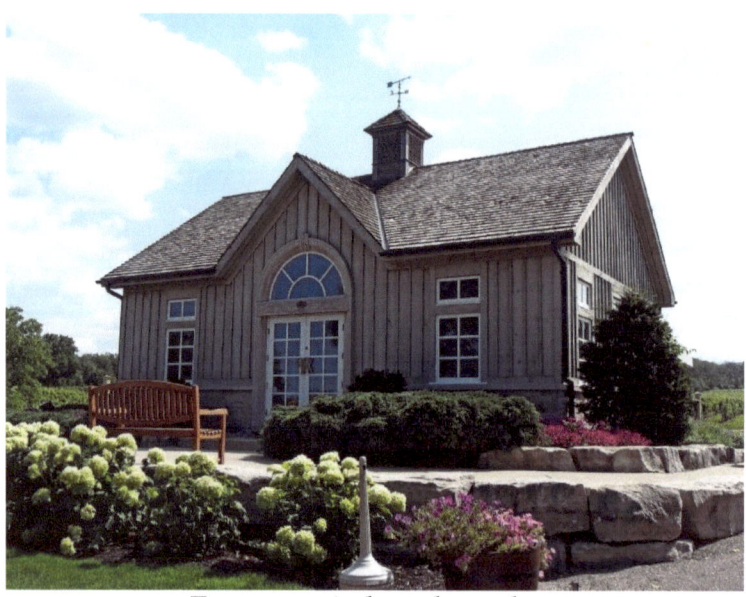

Transom window above door

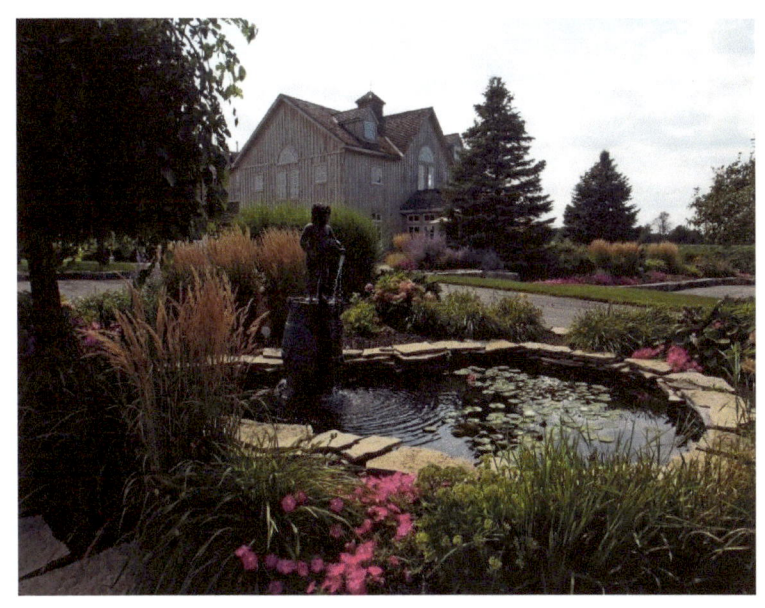

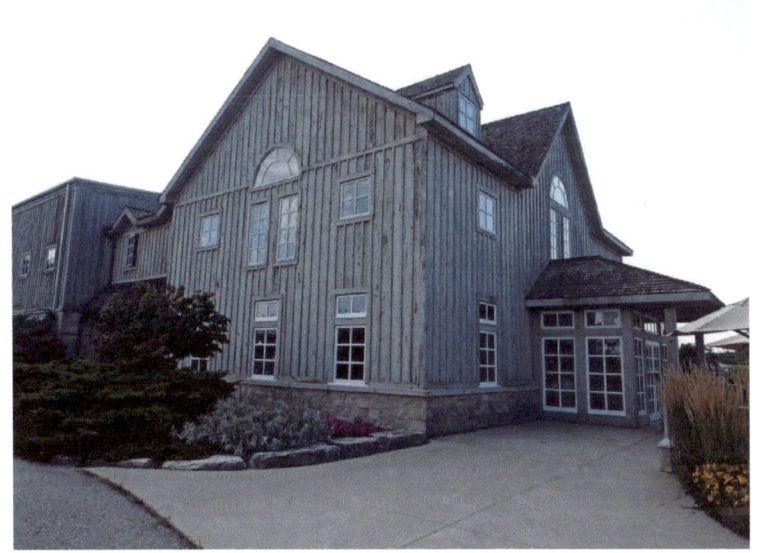

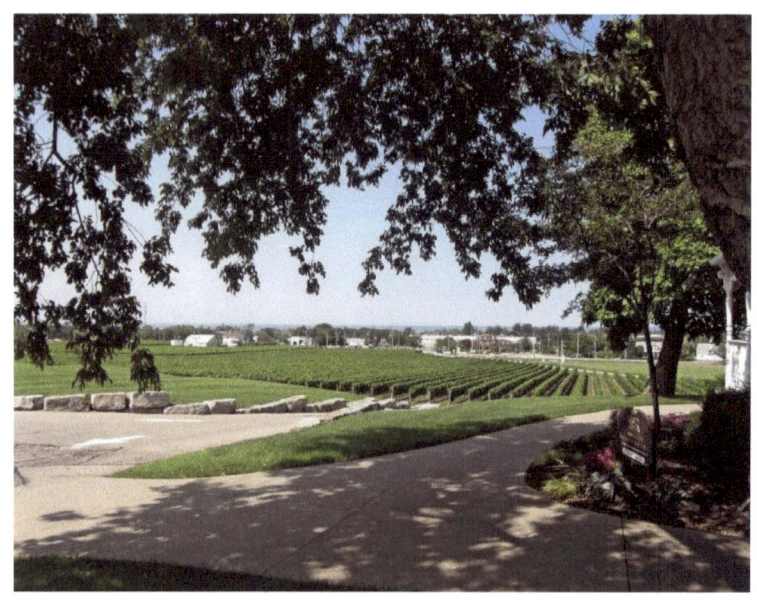

Vineyard

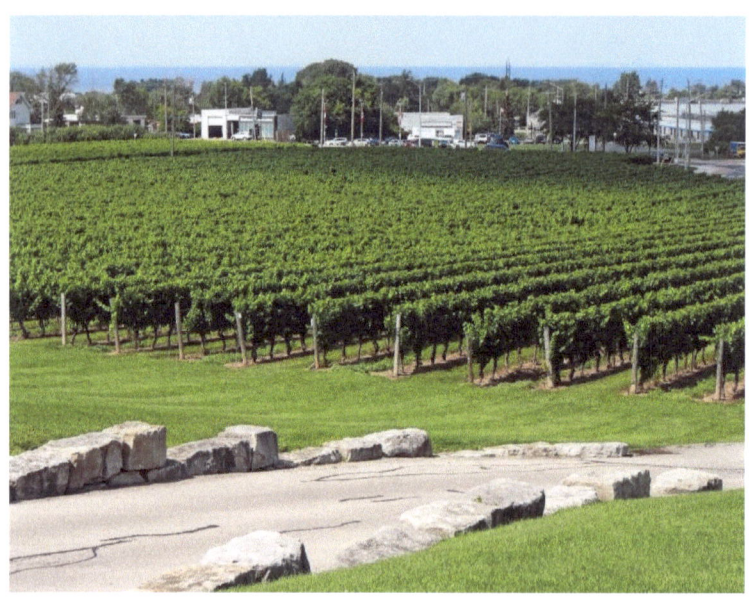

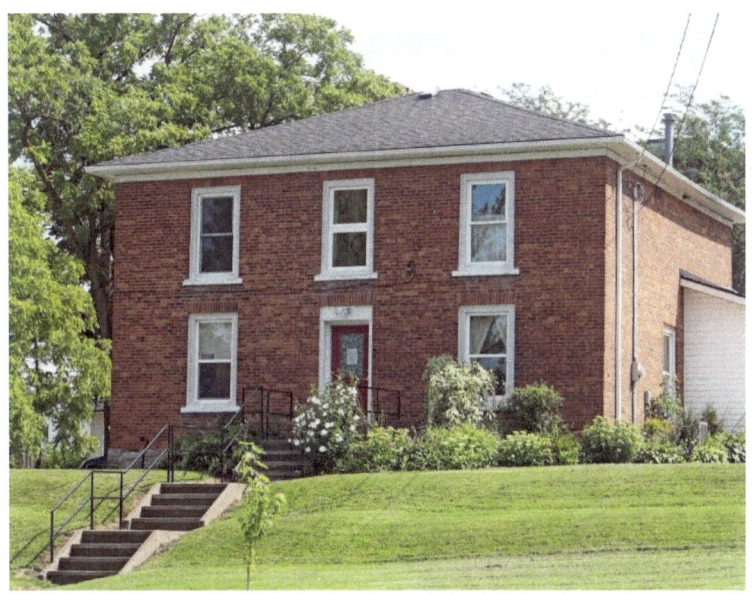

King Street – hipped roof, balanced façade

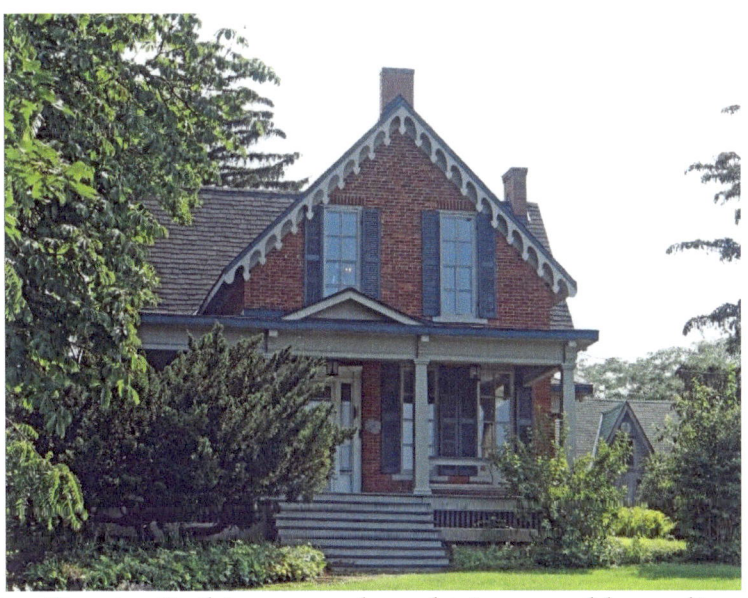

King Street – Gothic – verge board trim on gable, pediment

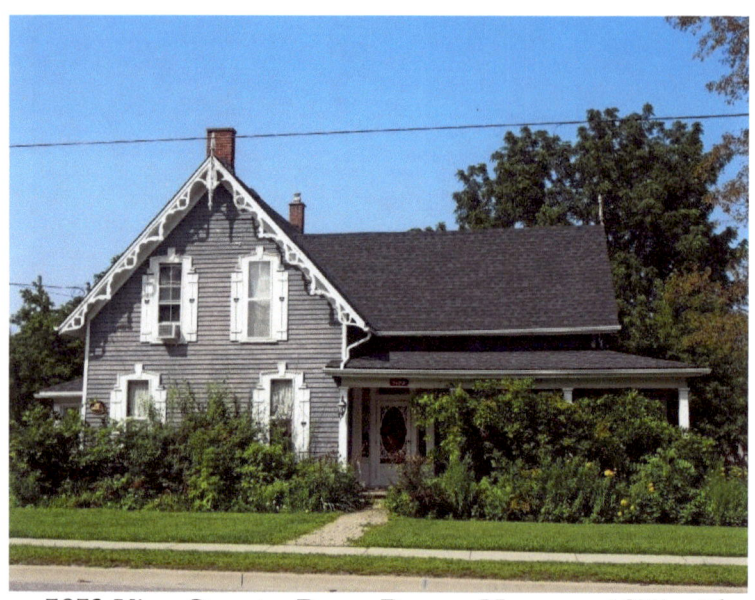

5053 King Street – Beam Barnes House c. 1855 – The property was originally granted by the Crown to Samuel Corwin in 1803. His wife was Anna Beam, daughter of Loyalist pioneer Jacob Beam. Her brother, Jacob Beam Jr. built the house between 1852 and 1855. The frame house is an early version of the Gothic Revival style. Notable features are steeply pitched gable roofs with carved finials and cut out quatrefoils worked into the barge board on both the front façade and east wing. The veranda has simple square posts, and the front door has a paned transom and sidelights. The tops of the slender but widely framed windows are surrounded with shaped lintels and decorative keystones.

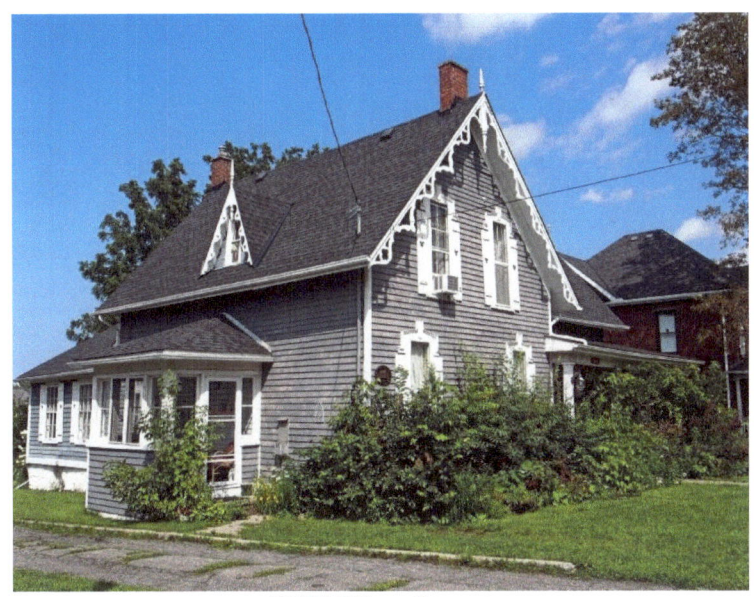

5053 King Street

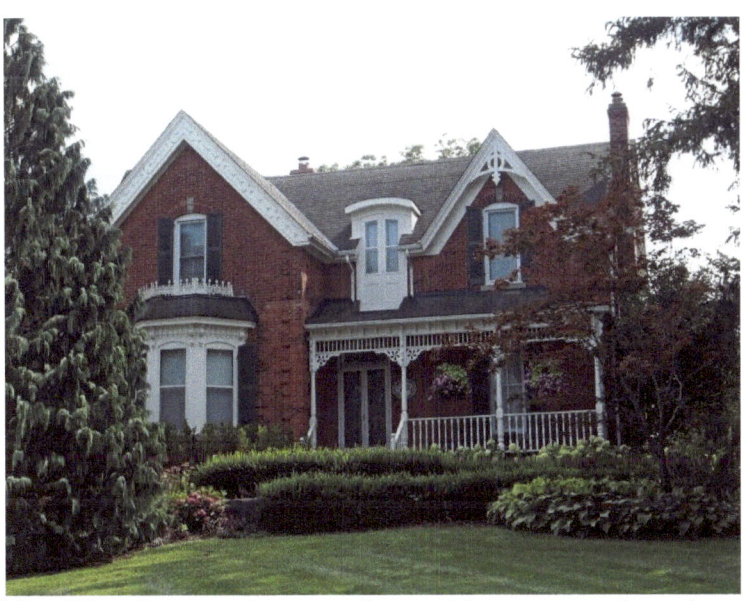

5074 King Street – bay window with iron cresting above

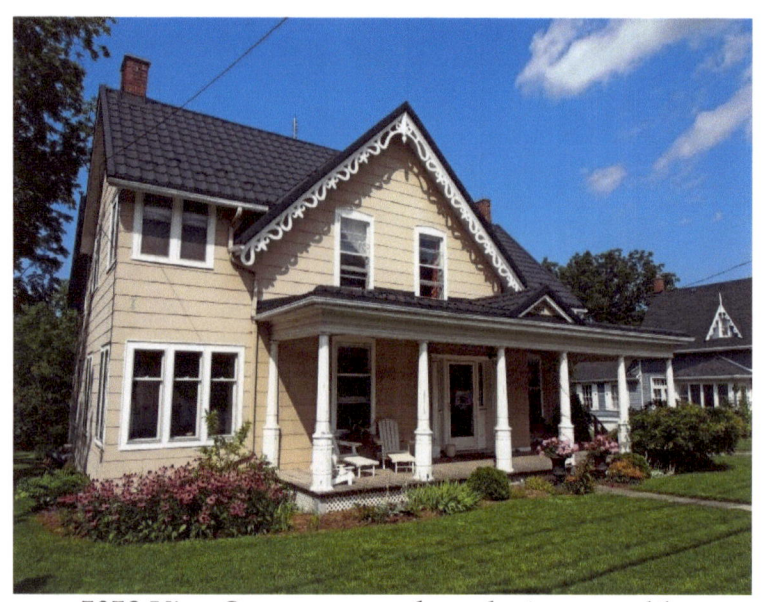

5059 King Street – verge board trim on gable

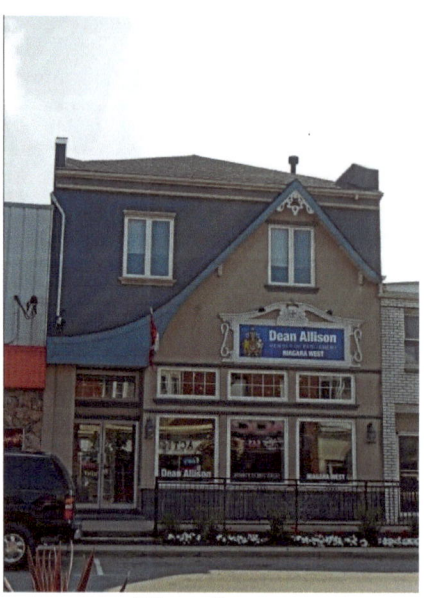

King Street

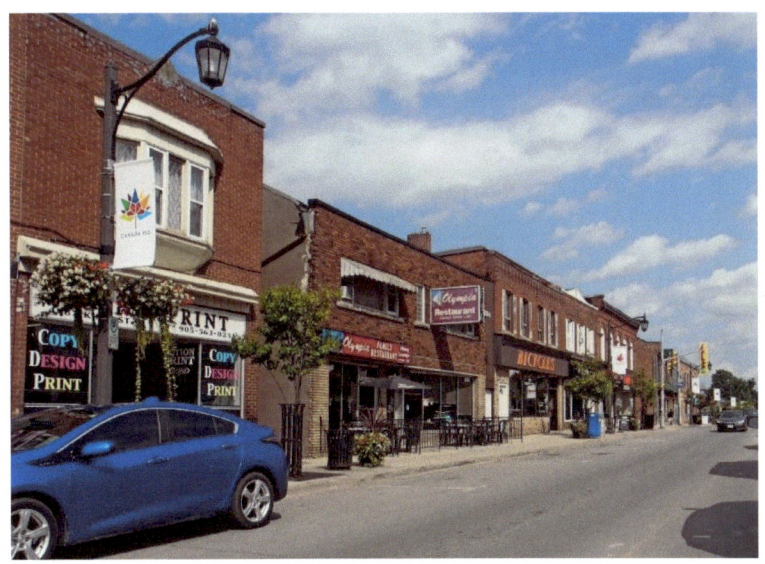

King Street

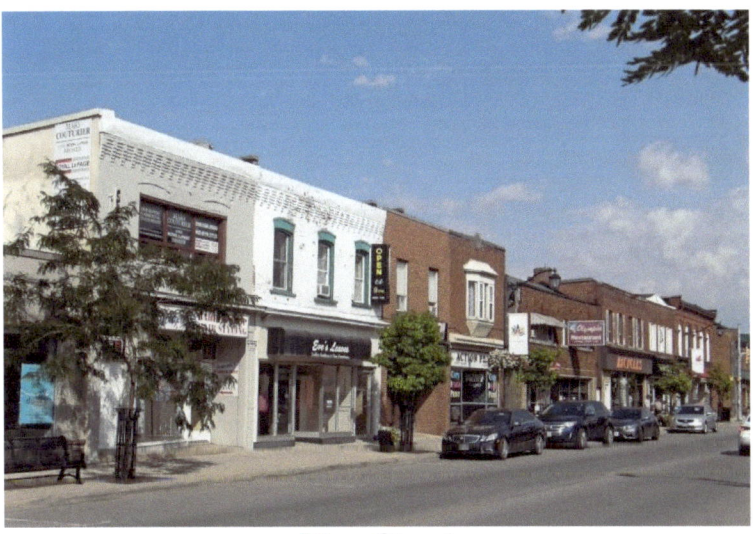

King Street

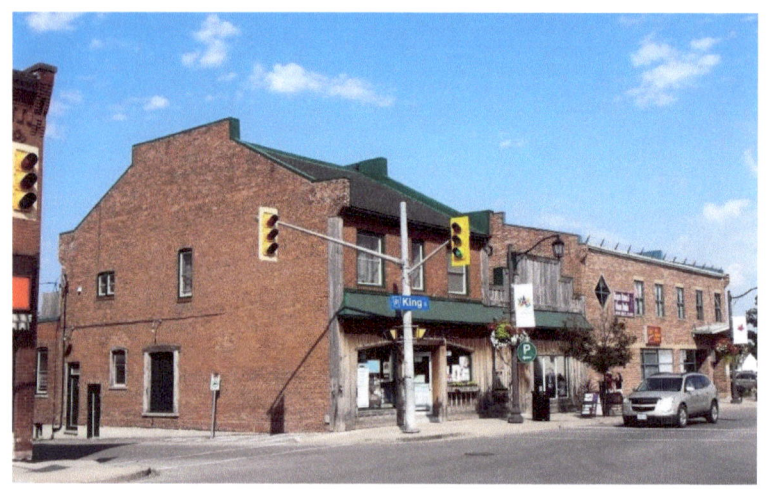
King Street

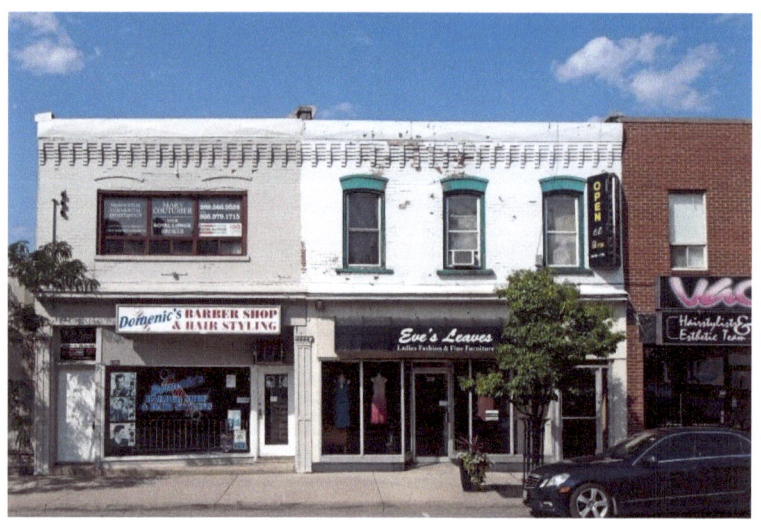
4991-4993 King Street – bevelled dentil molding

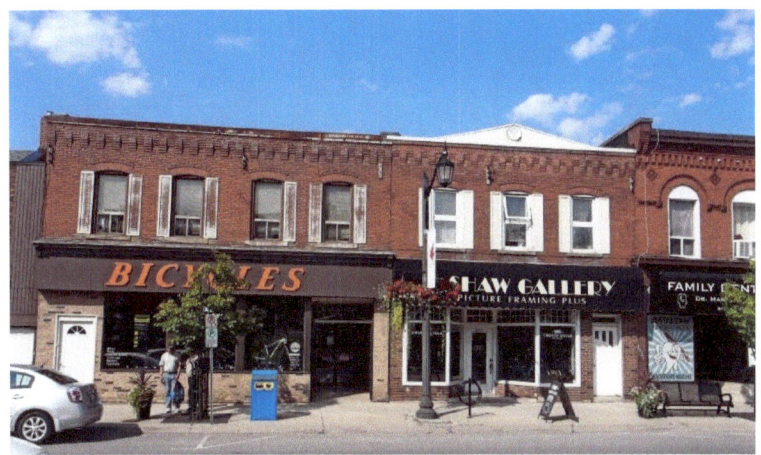

4977-4979 King Street

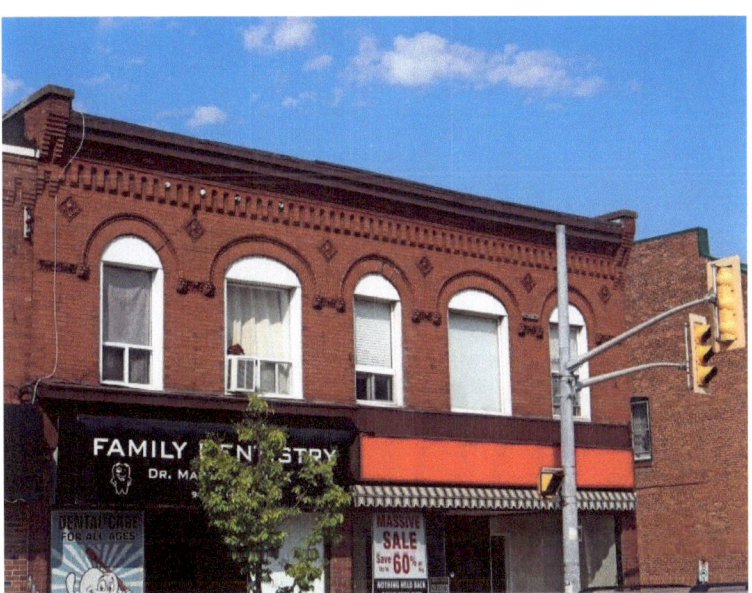

4975 King Street

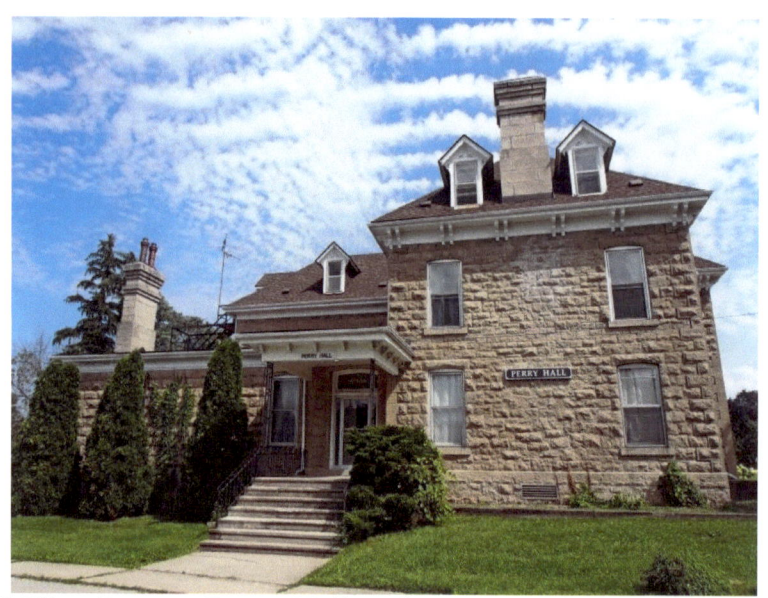

5545 King Street – Perry Hall – The Great Lakes Christian College is run out of the former home of Senator Gibson which was built circa 1890.

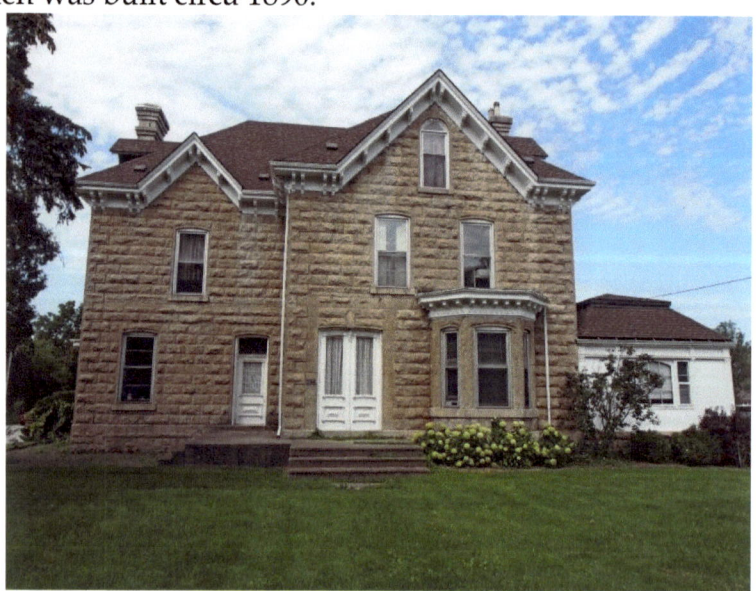

Cornice brackets, bay window

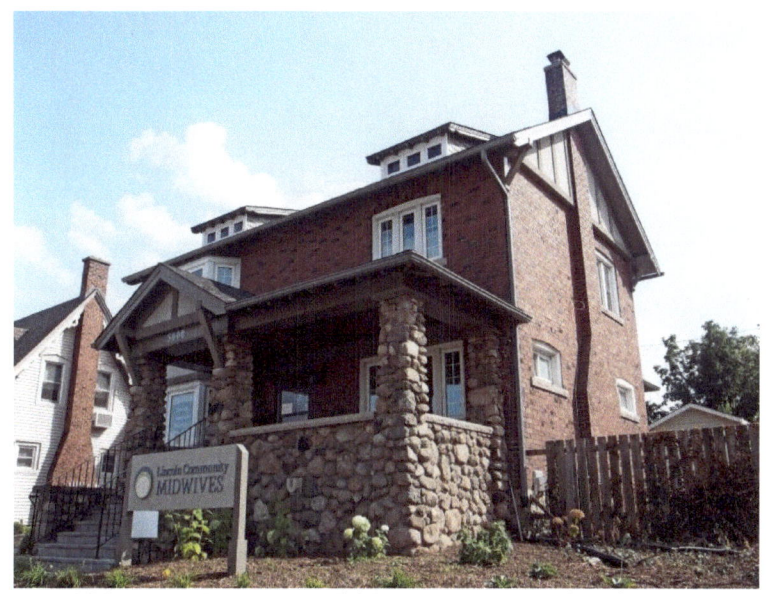

5000 King Street – cobblestone veranda, dormers

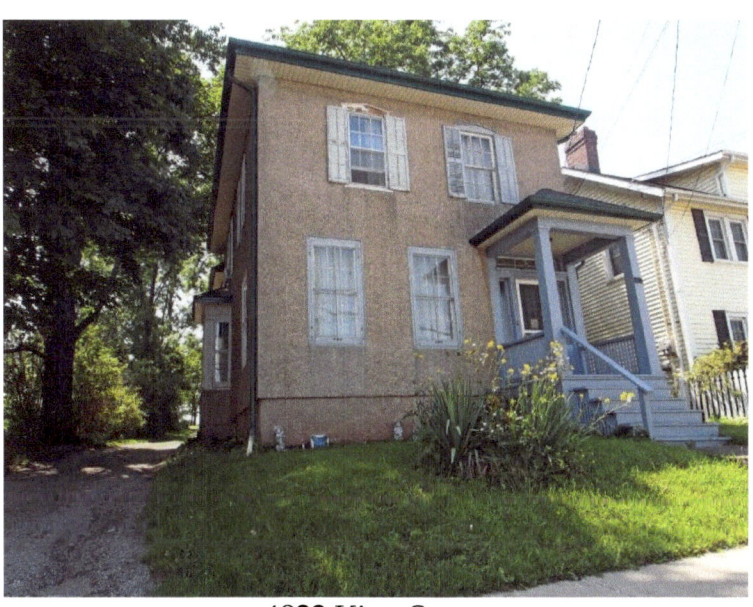

4922 King Street

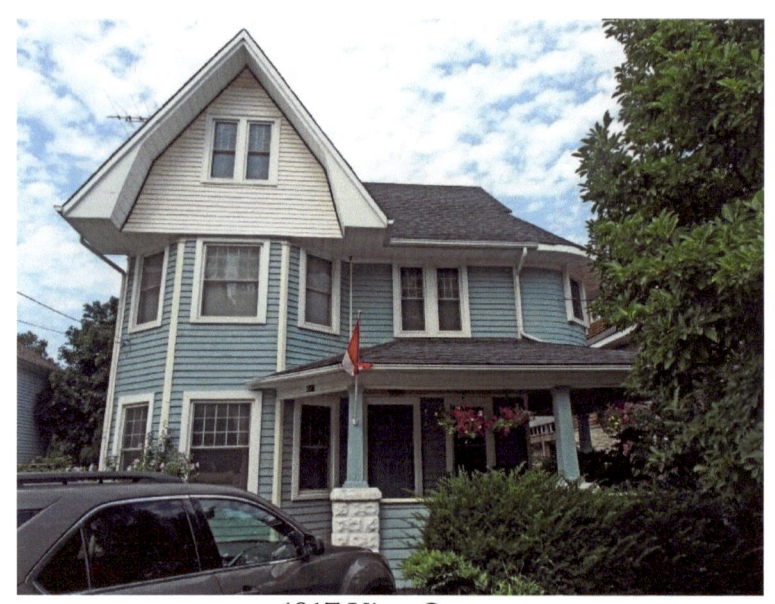

4917 King Street

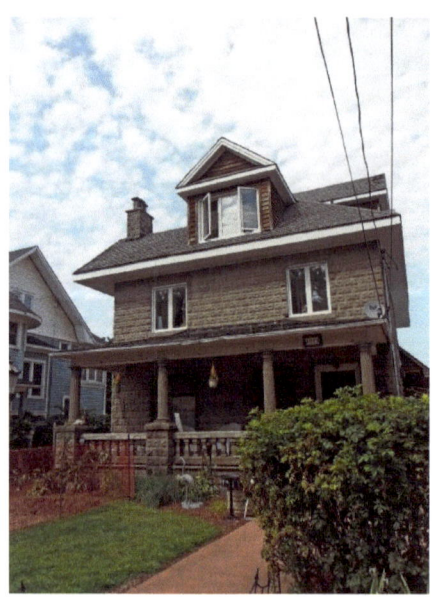

4915 King Street - dormer

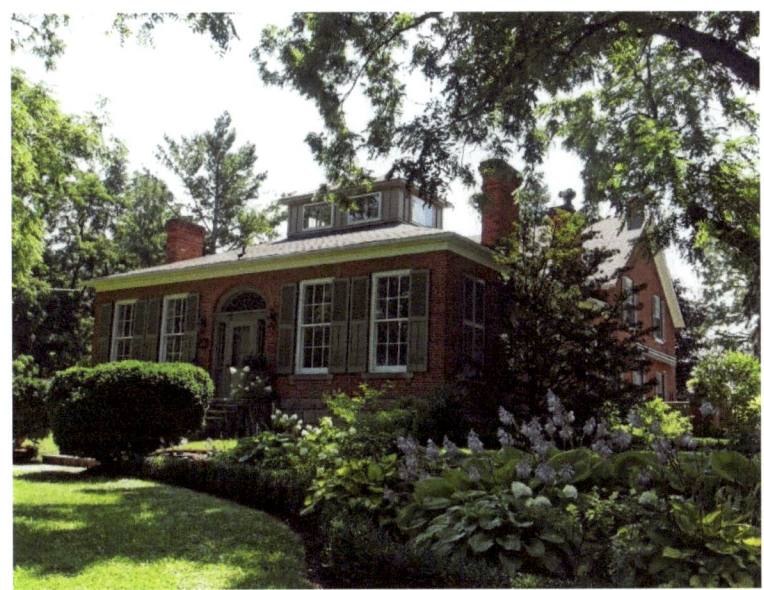

4918 King Street – Woodburn Cottage - The land was originally deeded by Crown Patent to Jacob Beam in 1801. The house built about 1834 for James B. Osborne, a merchant, postmaster and private banker. He was a prominent member of the community. The name "Woodburn" is said to have derived from James Osborne's second wife's family. The house is Regency Cottage in style. It is built of Flemish double stretcher bond red brick on top of a fieldstone foundation. The front façade has an impressive double door with sidelights and a fan transom housed in an arched brick surround. Flanking the doorway are four large, shuttered windows, each with twelve panes and flat stone lintels on top. The hipped roof has double-flued, corbeled chimneys on each corner and has a large belvedere on top.

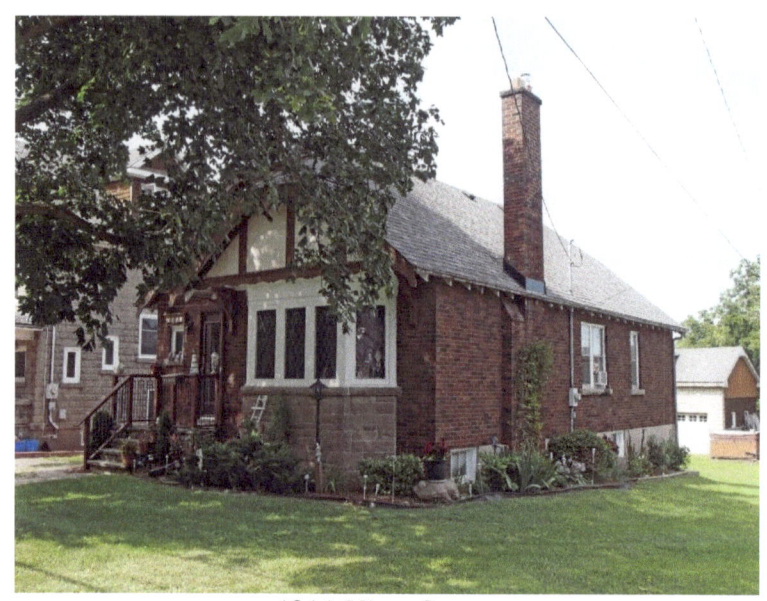

4911 King Street

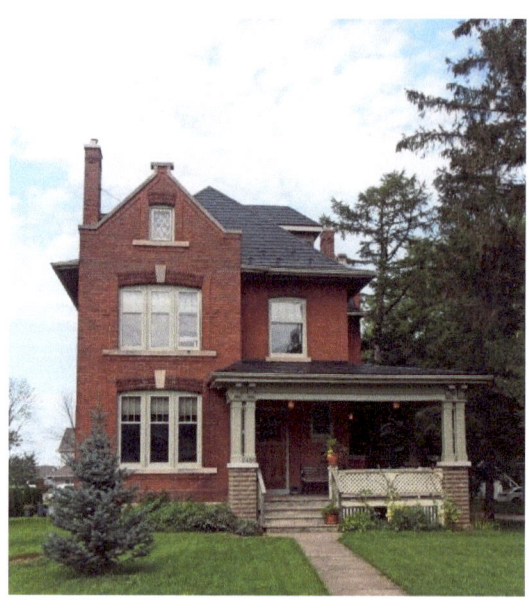

4881 King Street – voussoirs, keystones

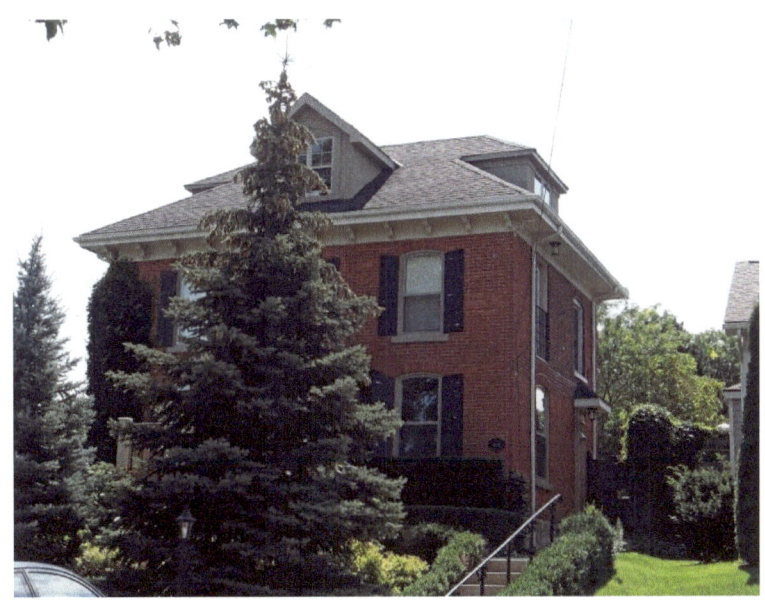
4866 King Street - dormers

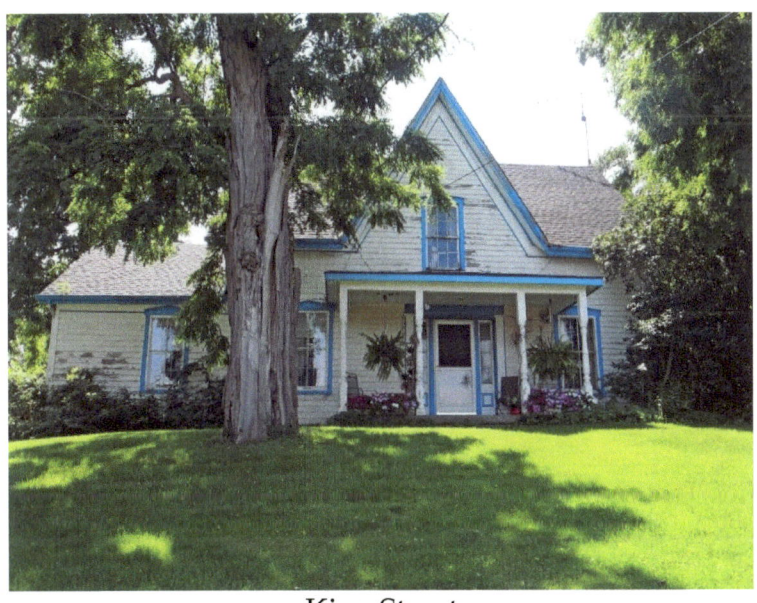
King Street

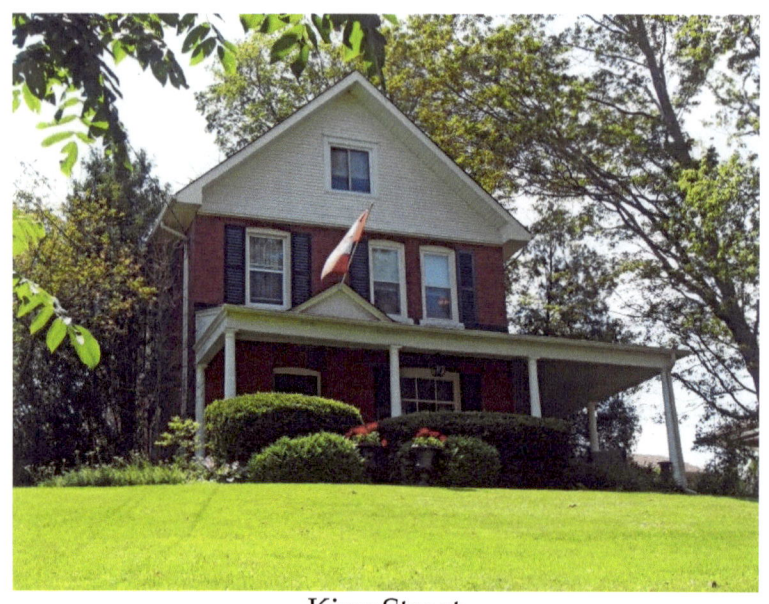

King Street

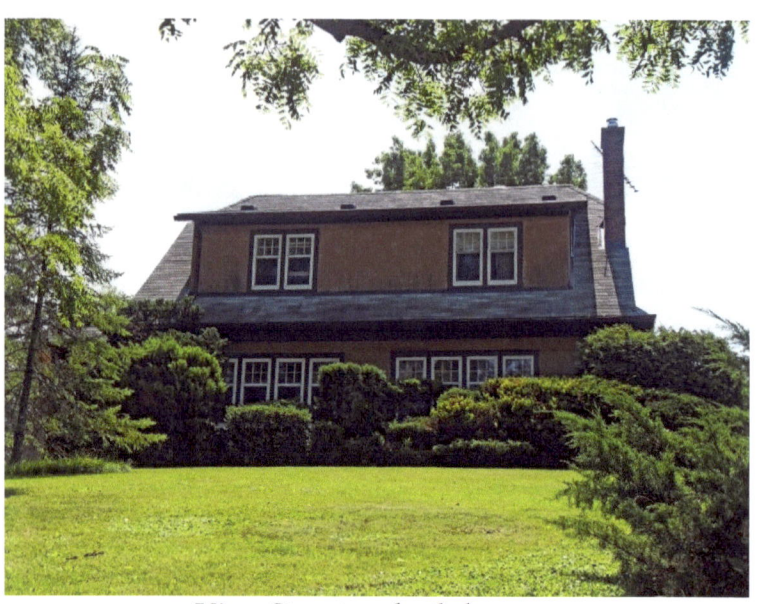

King Street – shed dormer

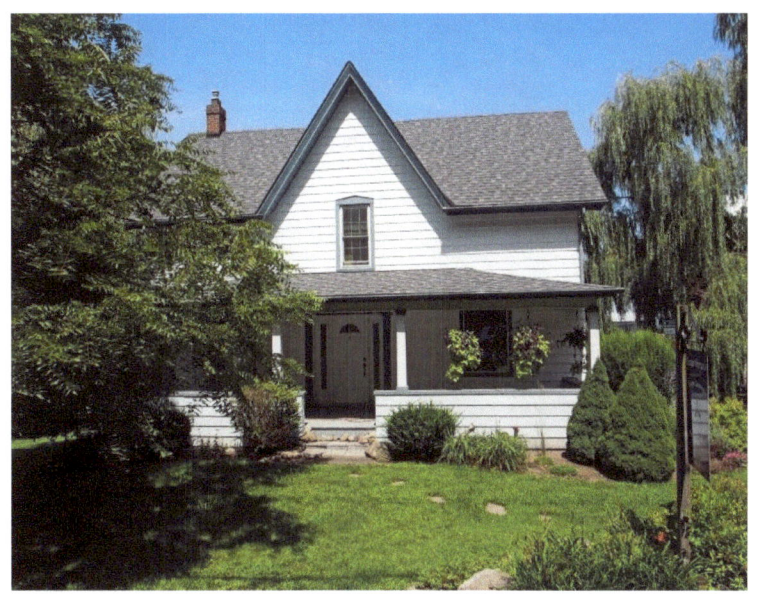

King Street – Regency Cottage

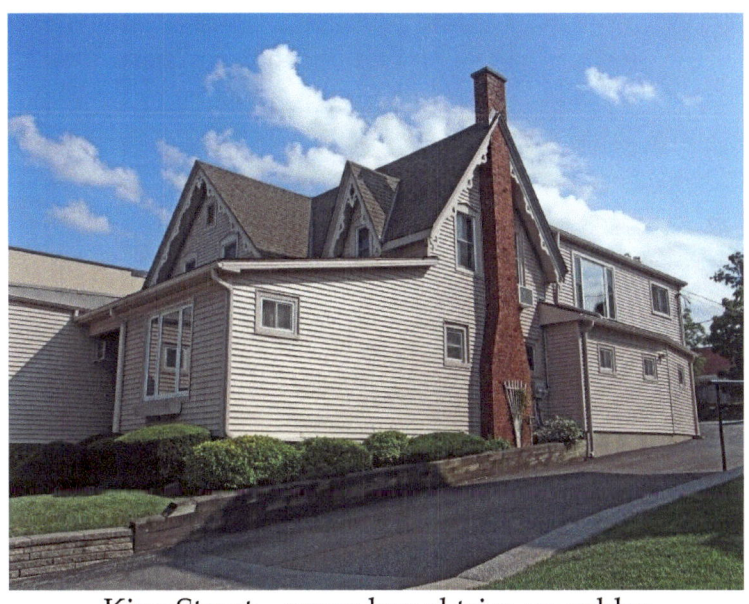

King Street – verge board trim on gables

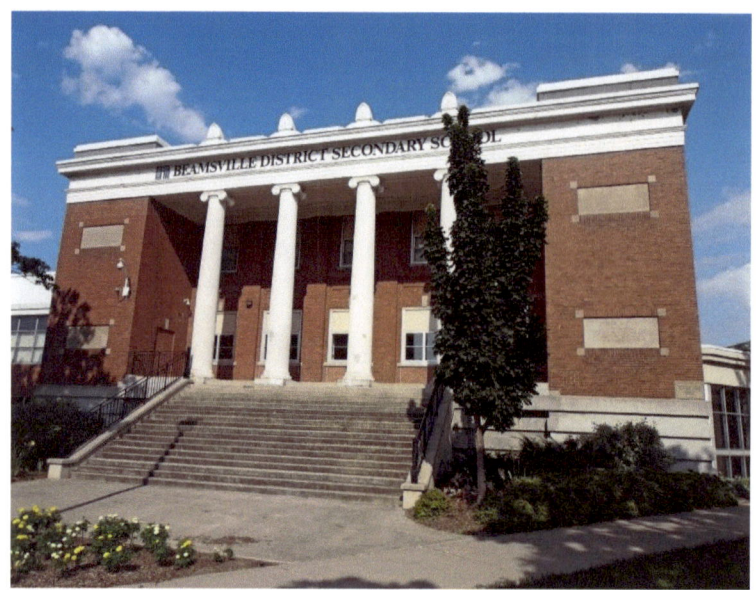

4317 Central Avenue – Beamsville District High School – erected 1917 – Class of 2000 – Give the world the best you have and the best will come back to you. The end of education is character, and the test of character is service. Wisdom is the principal thing; therefore, get wisdom – Proverbs 4:7. Ionic capitals

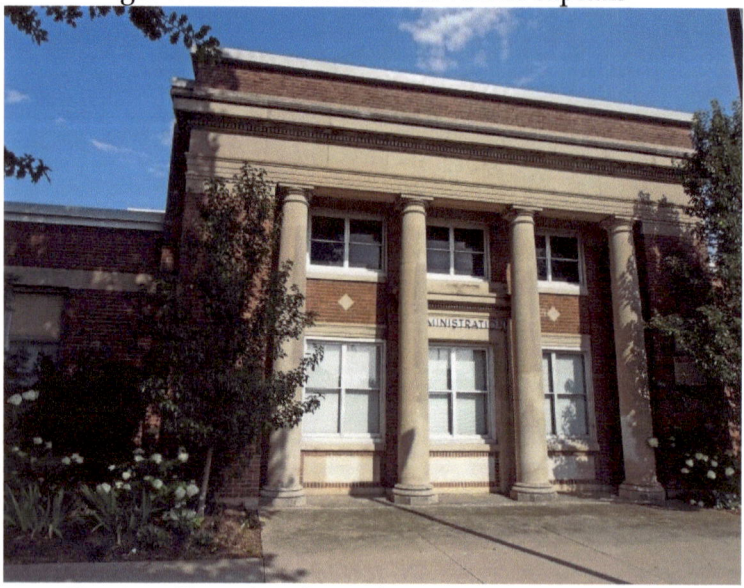

Doric pillars for the Administration building

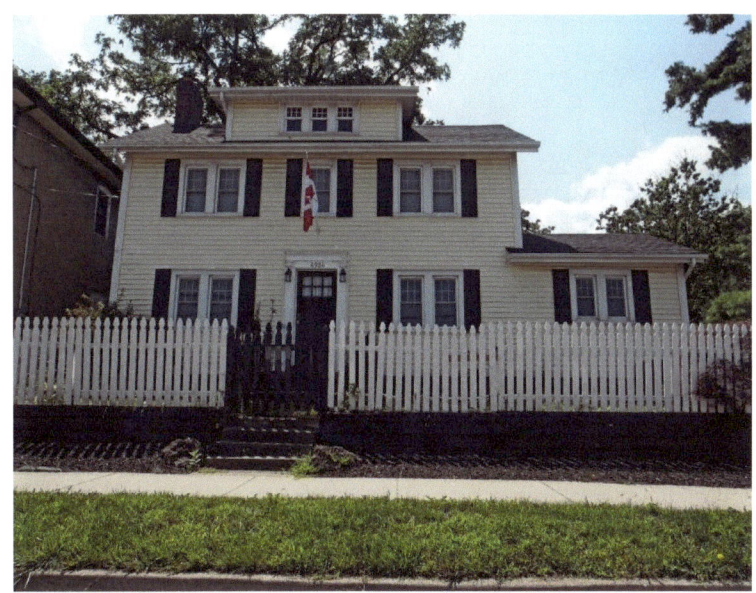

4294 King Street – two-storeys with dormer above, balanced façade

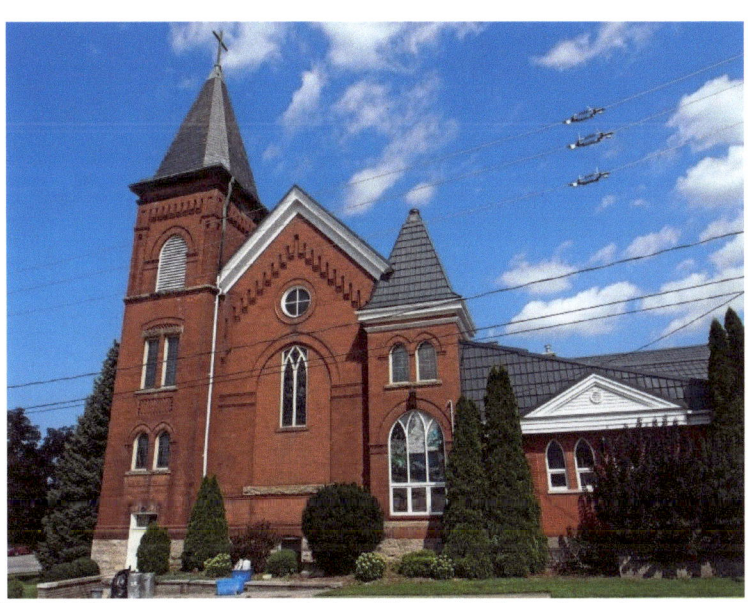

4287 William Street – Trinity United Church – three-storey tower - 1898

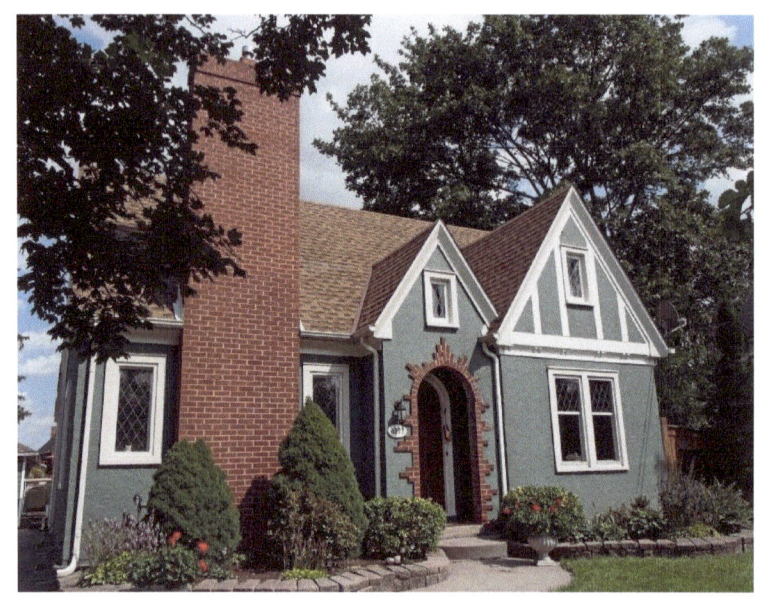
4277 William Street

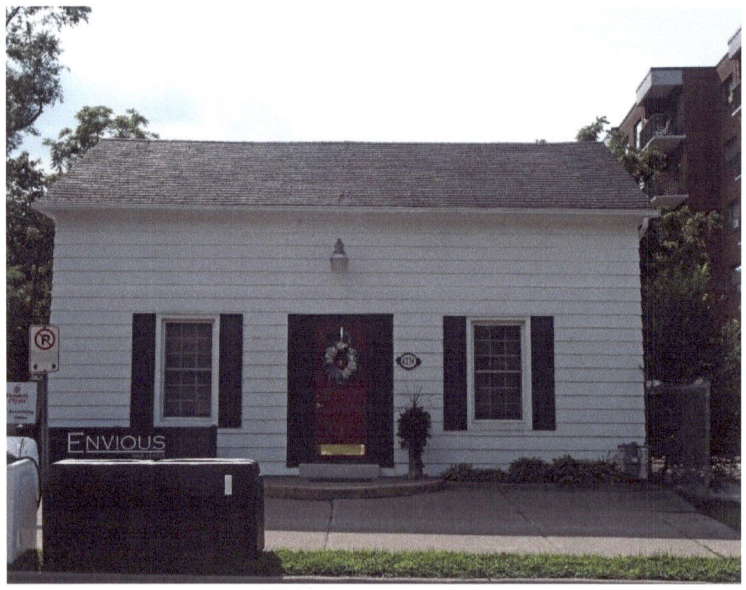
4274 Queen Street

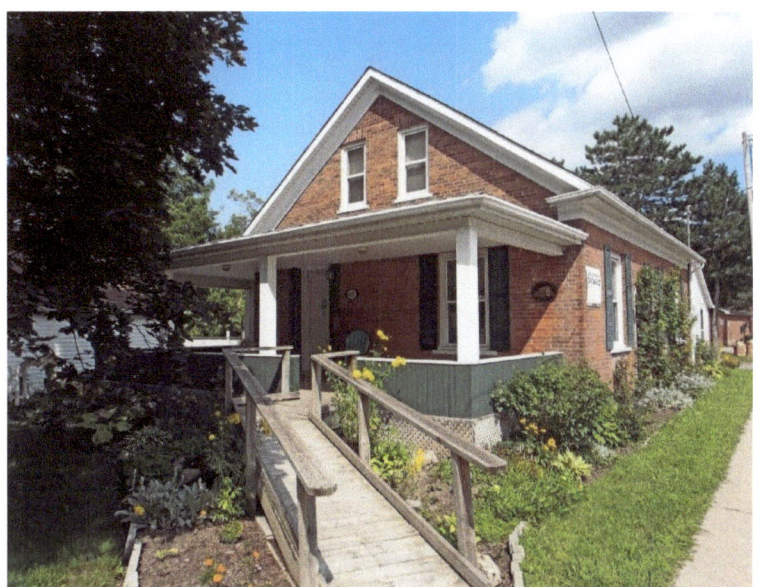

4271 Queen Street - Originally built as a school in 1847, the house is supported by a rubble stone foundation and hand-hewn beams. The house has a pitched gable roof and large double-hung windows. There are two pairs of smaller windows in both the front and back gables. It is now the Adult Learning & Resource Center for Niagara West.

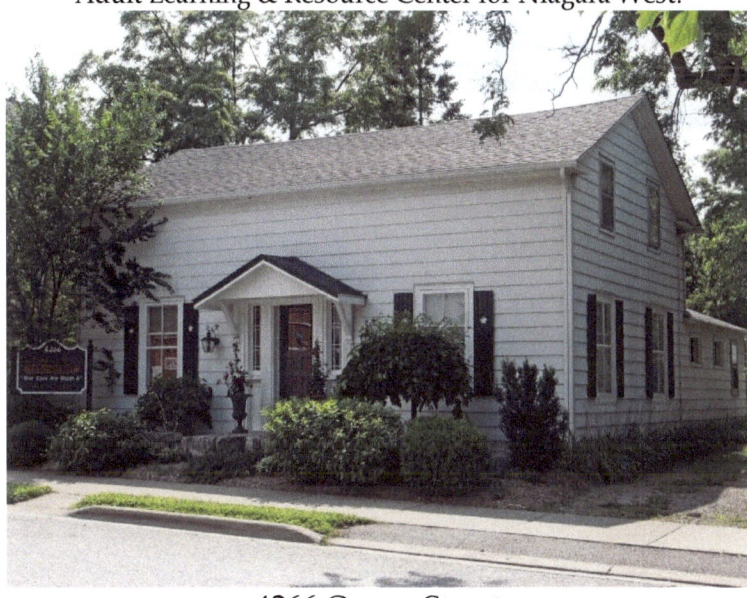

4266 Queen Street

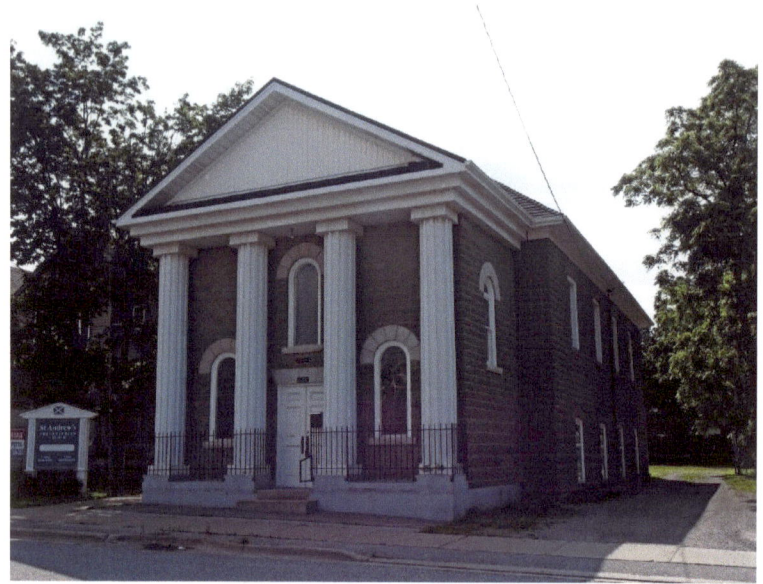

4260 Queen Street – St. Andrew's Presbyterian Church - Four pillars, with a pediment above, hold up the front of the roof.

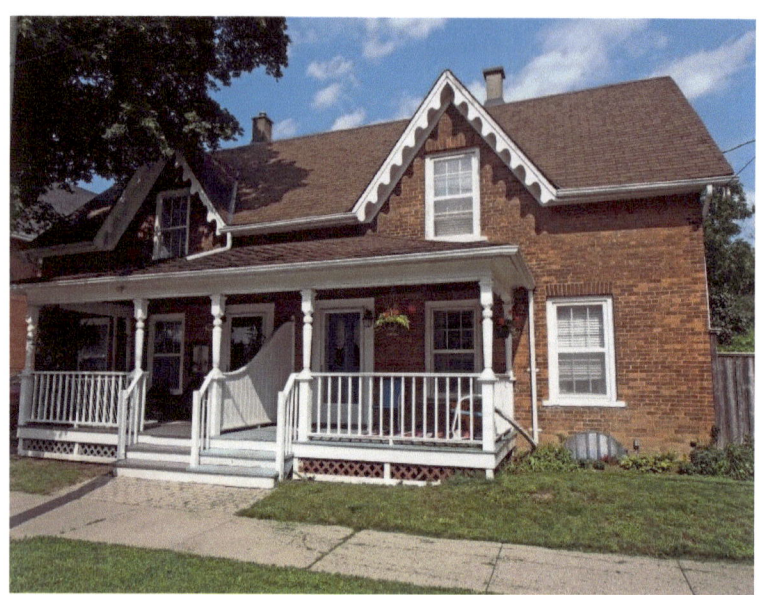

4275-4279 Queen Street – Gothic Revival style, verge board trim on gables

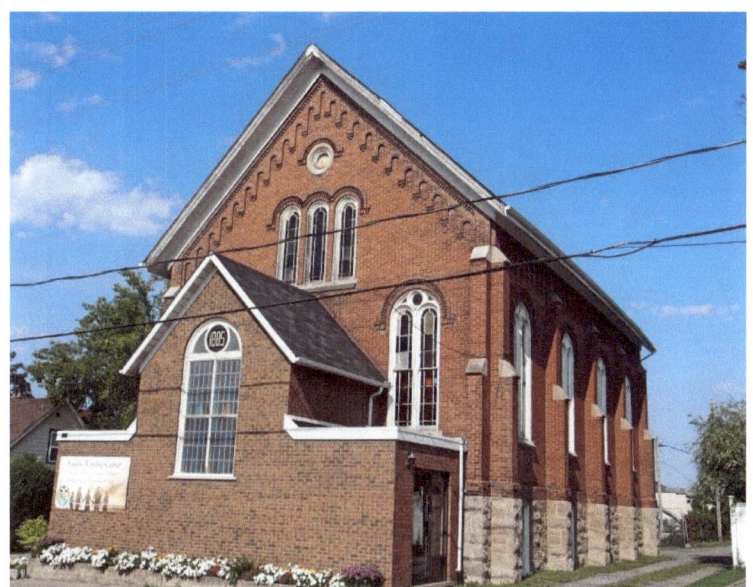

4281 Queen Street – Family Worship Center – buttresses, bevelled dentil molding

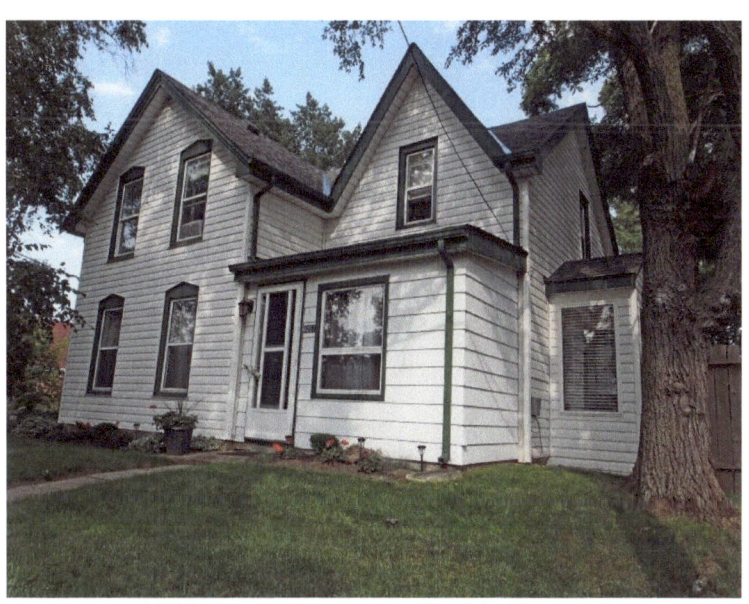

4251 Queen Street – Gothic Revival

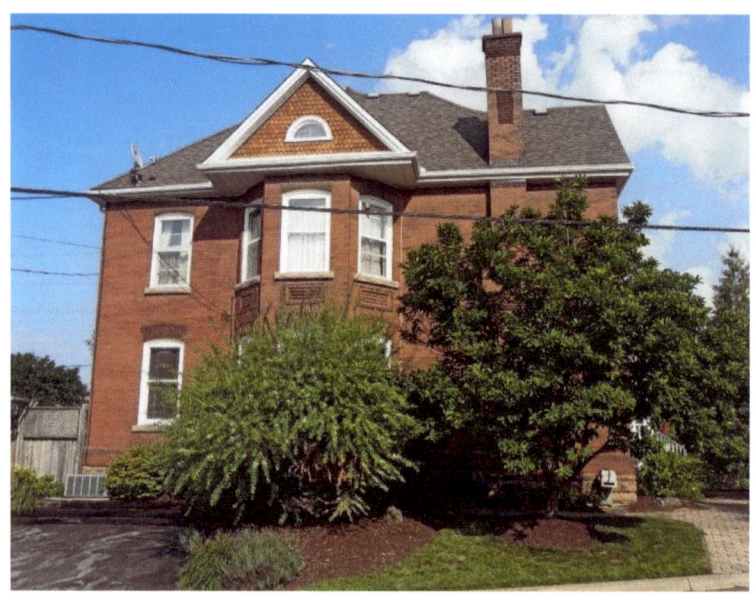

Queen Street – 2½ storey bay window, tall chimney

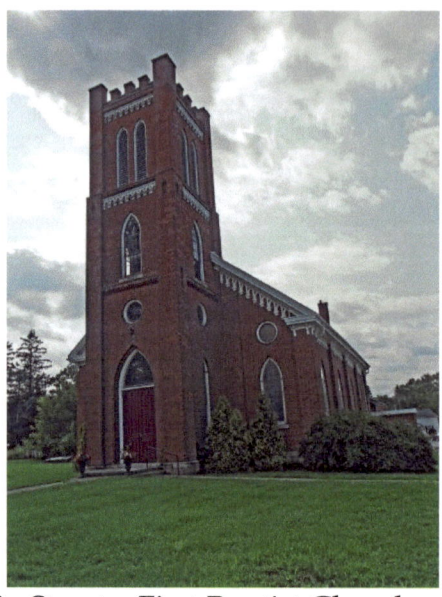

4264 Mountain Street – First Baptist Church – battlement at top of three-storey tower, lancet windows, rose window, decorative cornice with brackets, buttresses

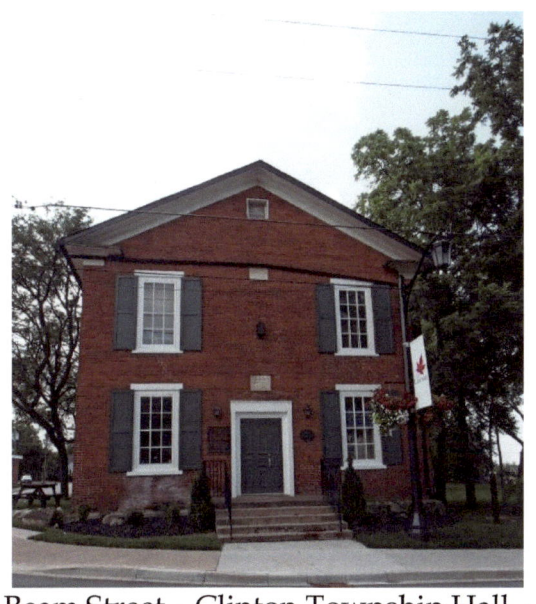

4996 Beam Street – Clinton Township Hall – 1851

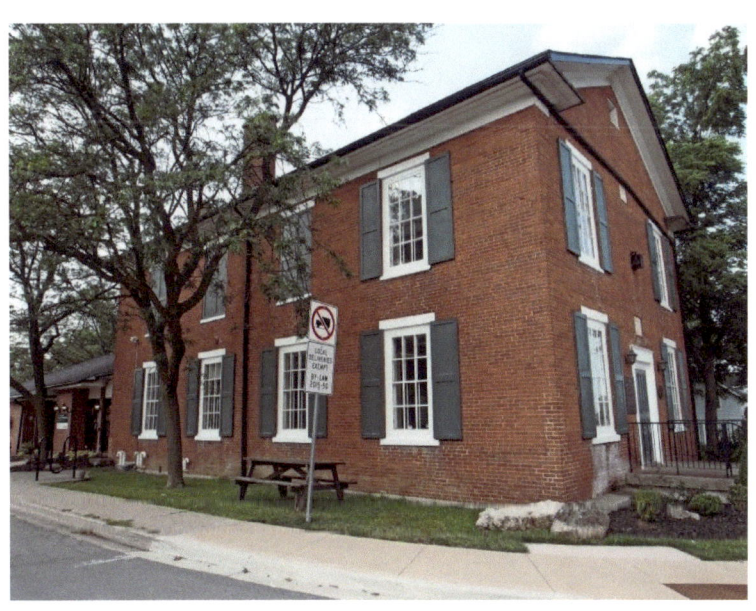

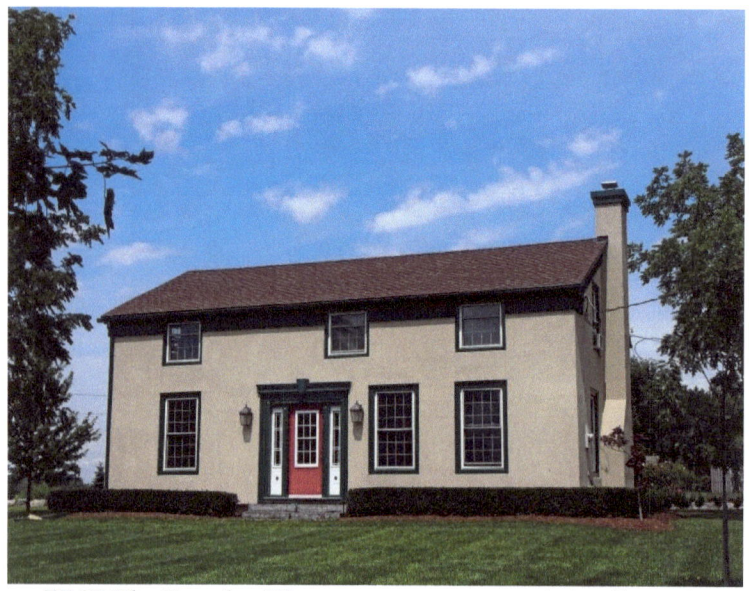

5567 Fly Road – The property was originally a Crown grant to Paul Marlatt in 1796. The Marlatts were part of the Huguenot migration from France to Virginia in the late 17th century. They moved to this area in the 1780s-1790s. James Durham bought the property in 1830 and he had the house built in 1832. The two-storey white stucco house has multiple-paned 12-over-12 windows and sidelights flanking either side of the front door.

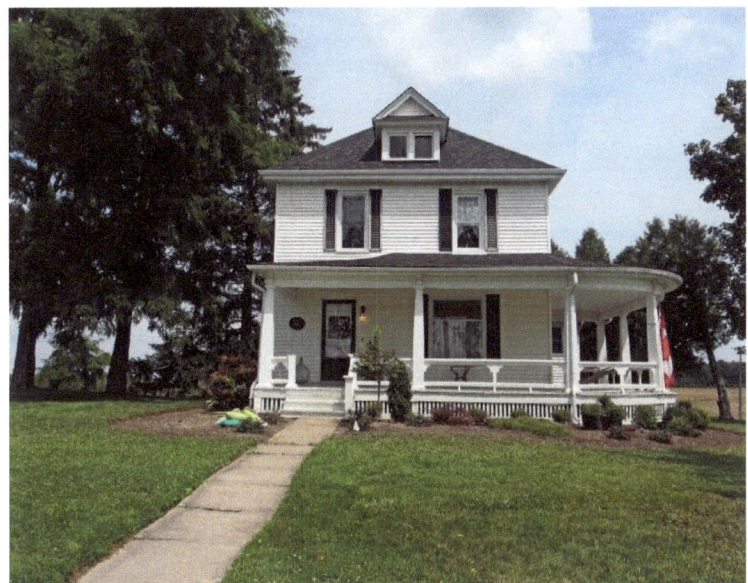

5031 Philp Road – Tufford Easton House – 1906 – Four-square asymmetrical 2½ storey house has a hip roof with a triangular-pediment-gabled dormer. It has a Queen Anne style wraparound veranda supported by seven square pillars.

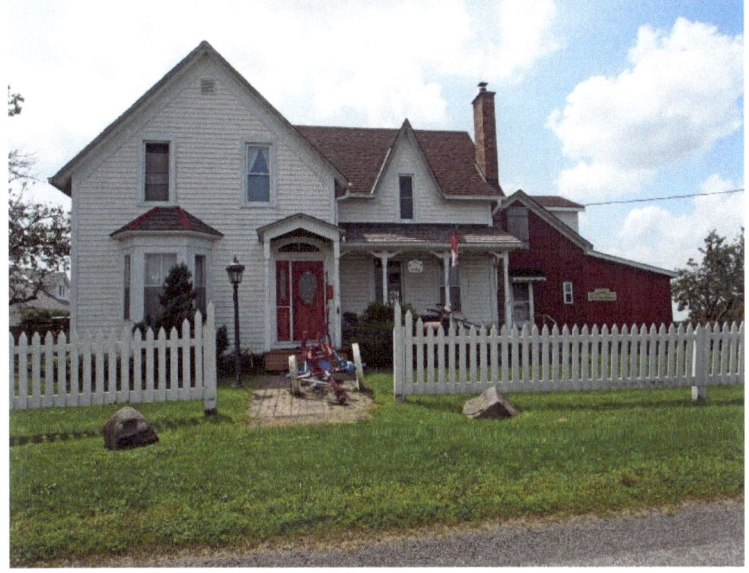

5128 Philp Road – Gothic, bay window, transom above door

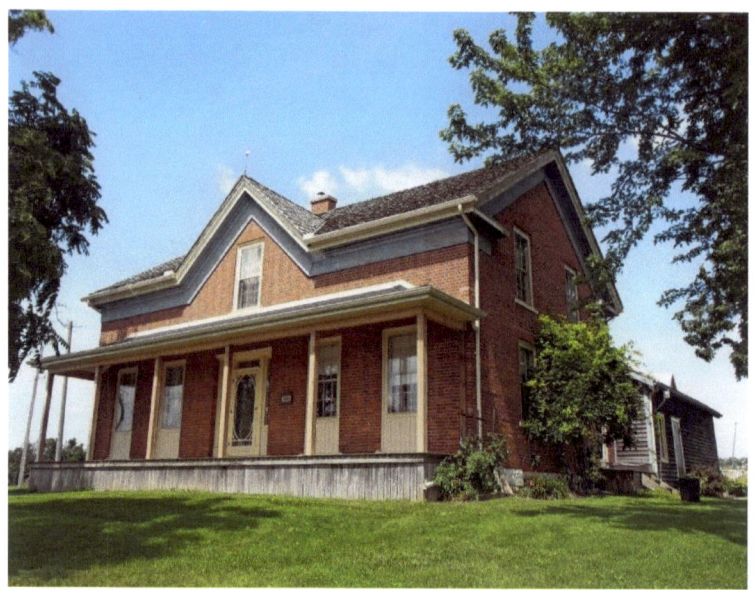

5499 Philp Road - The present house, of neoclassic vernacular design, dates to about 1850 and utilizes hand-hewn beams and Flemish and triple brick construction. The five bay façade has original windows and doors, with the front door flanked with sidelights and overhead transom. The main barn is a good unaltered example of an early 1800s Loyalist Barn in the English three bay style.

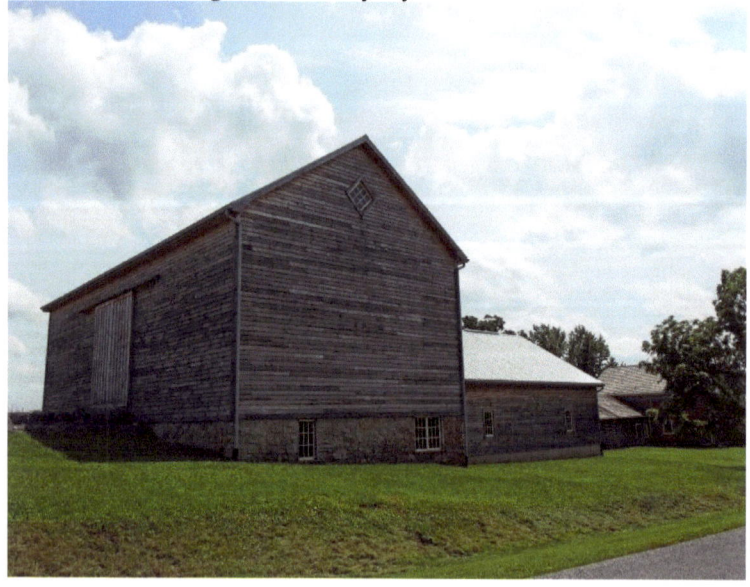

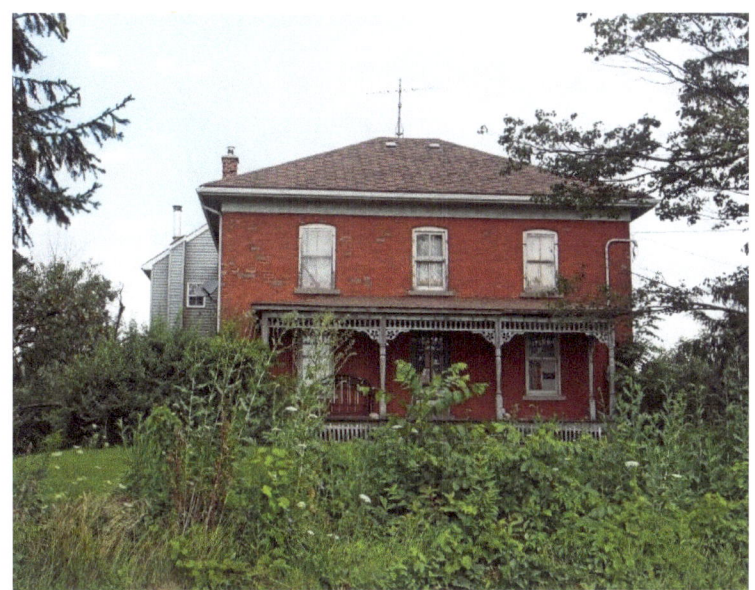

5257 Philp Road – hipped roof

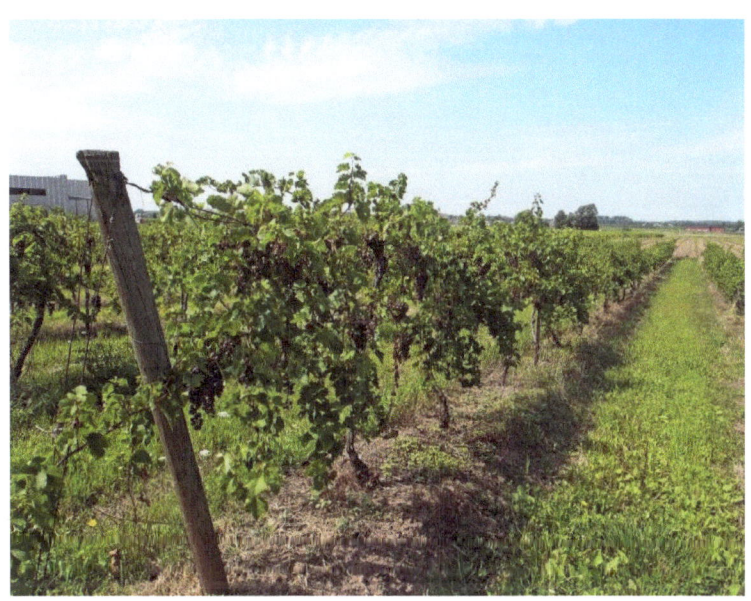

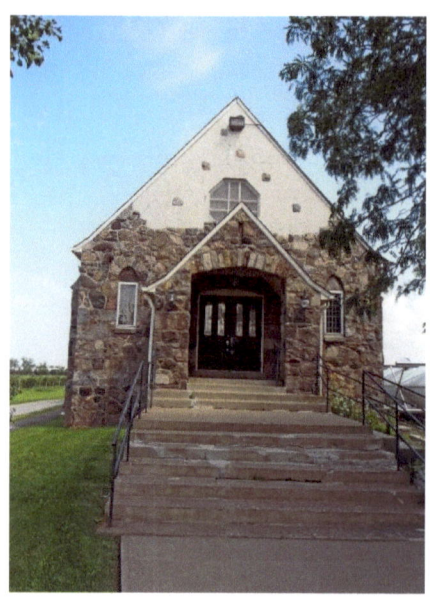

4157 Maple Grove Road – St. Helen Roman Catholic Church

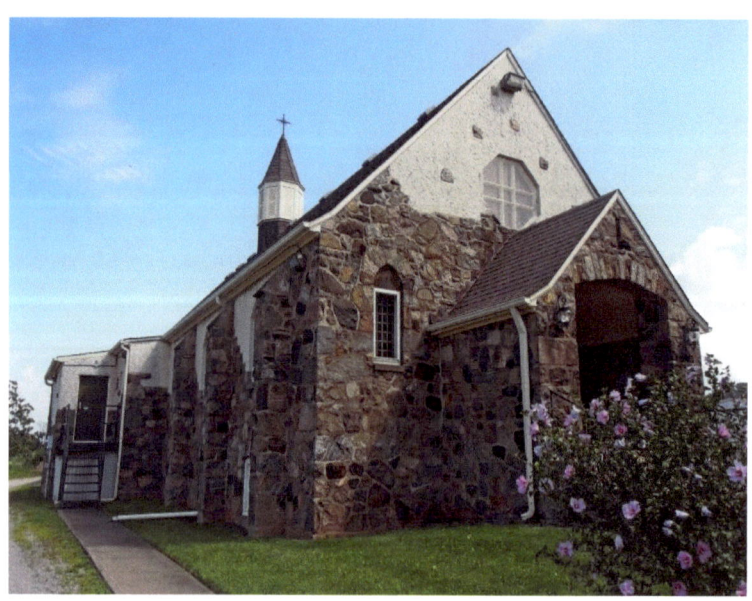

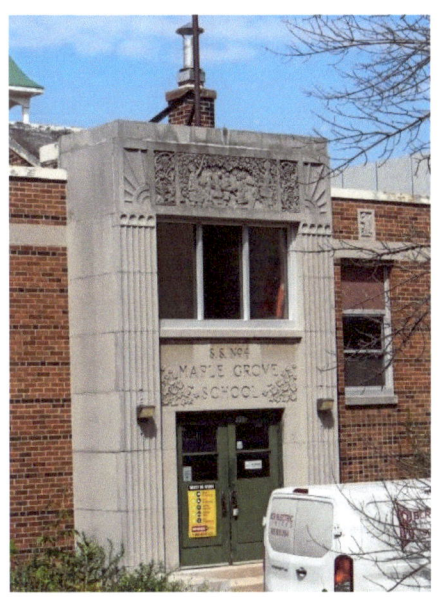

3991 Regional Road 81 - S. S. No. 4 Maple Grove School – closed in 2013 - future home of Bench Brewing Company

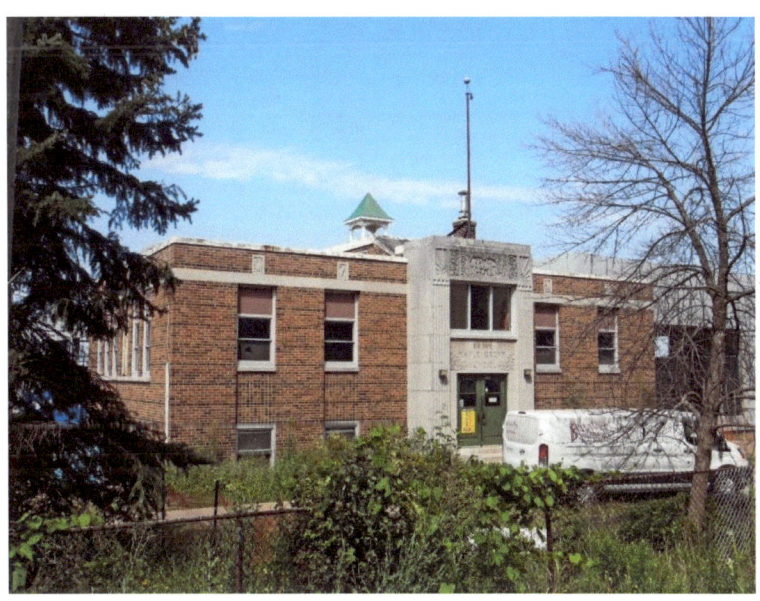

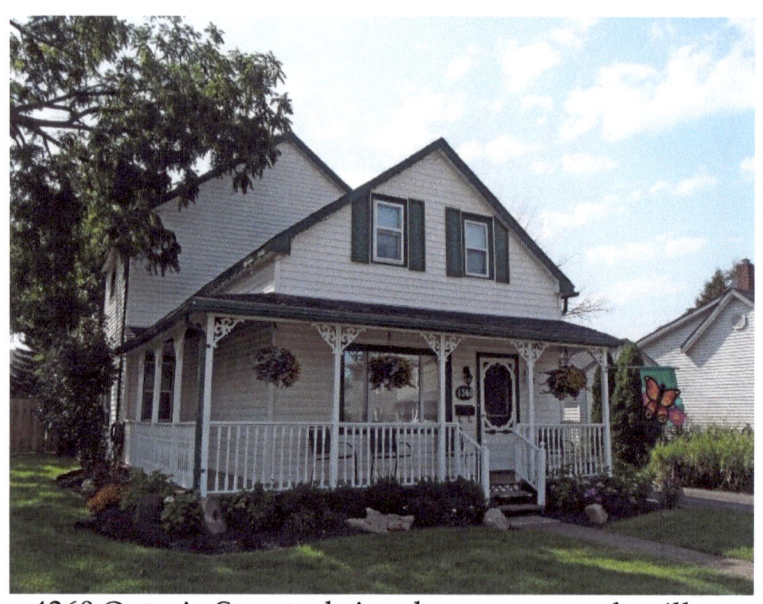

4360 Ontario Street – bric-a-brac on veranda pillars

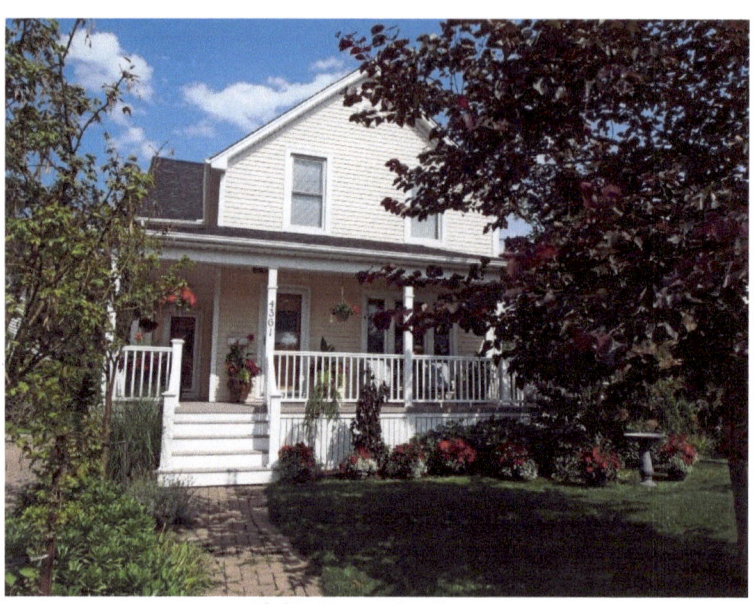

4361 Ontario Street

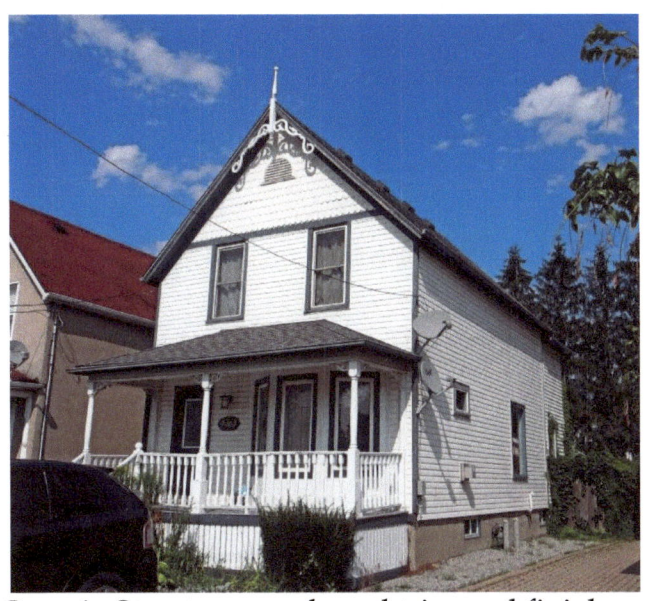

4363 Ontario Street – verge board trim and finial on gable

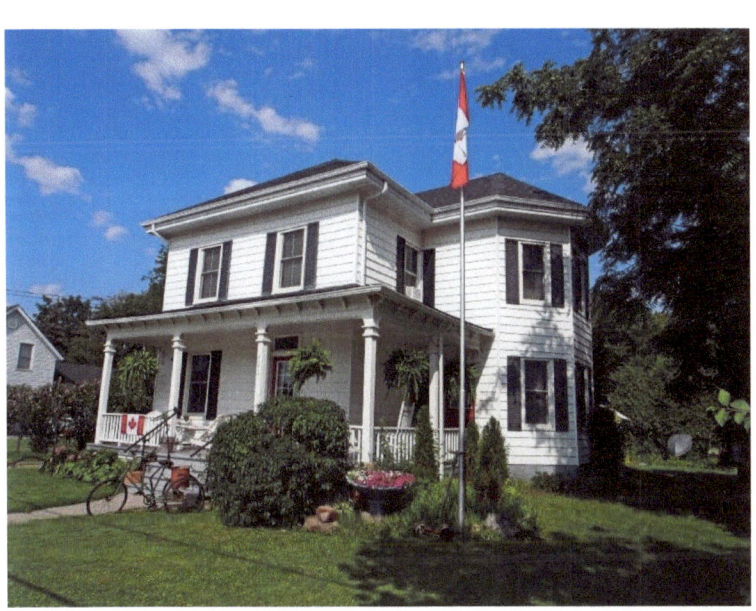

4373 Ontario Street

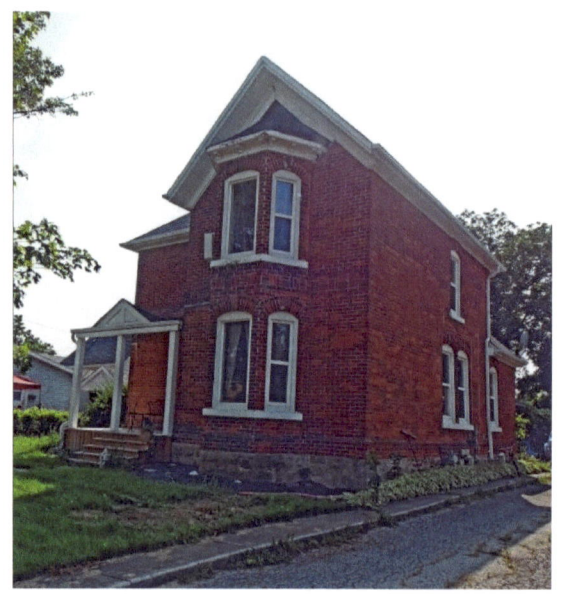

Ontario Street – two-storey bay window

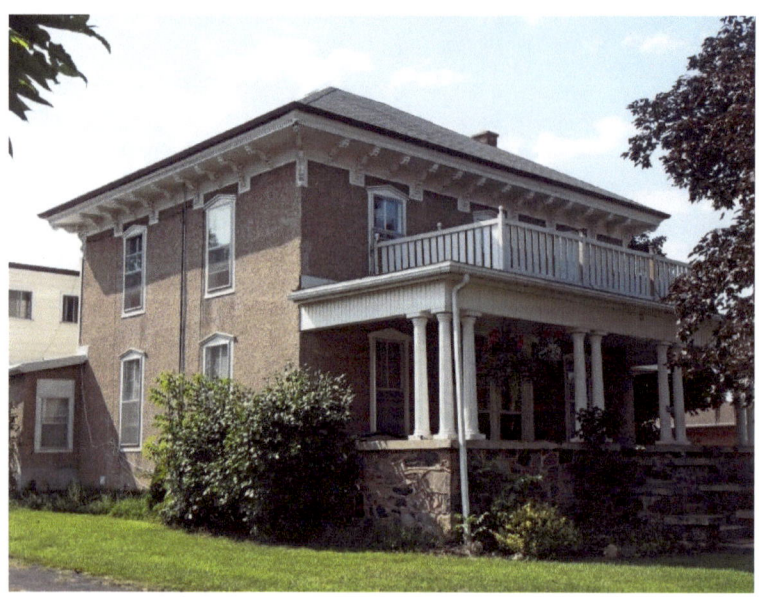

4382 Ontario Street – cornice brackets, second floor balcony

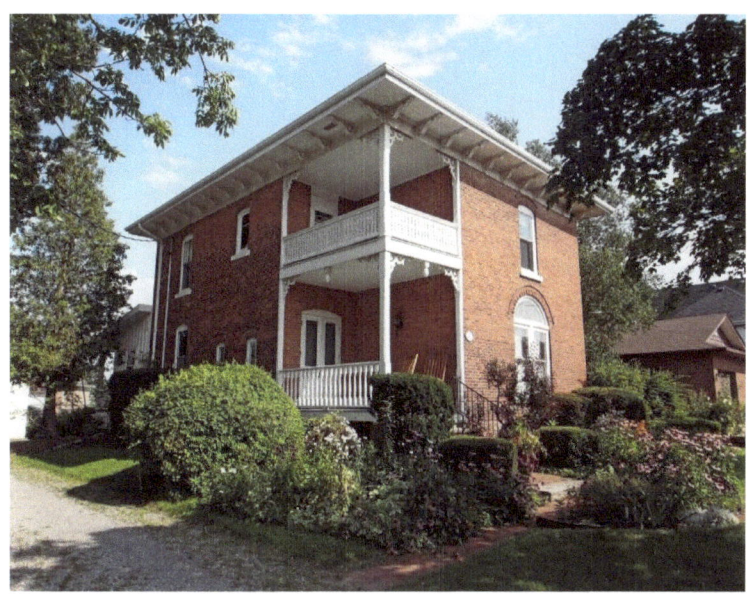

4351 Ontario Street – deep cornice with brackets, two-storey porch

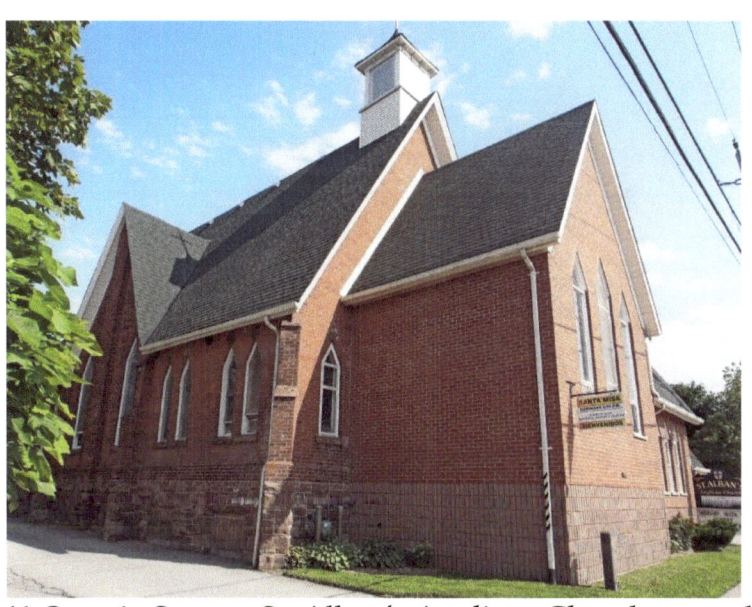

4341 Ontario Street – St. Alban's Anglican Church – cupola, lancet windows, buttresses

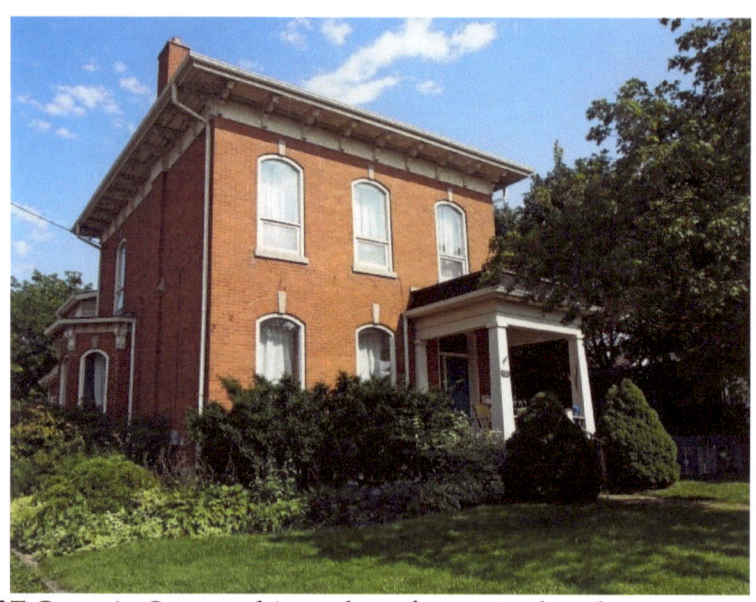

4337 Ontario Street – hipped roof, cornice brackets, voussoirs and keystones

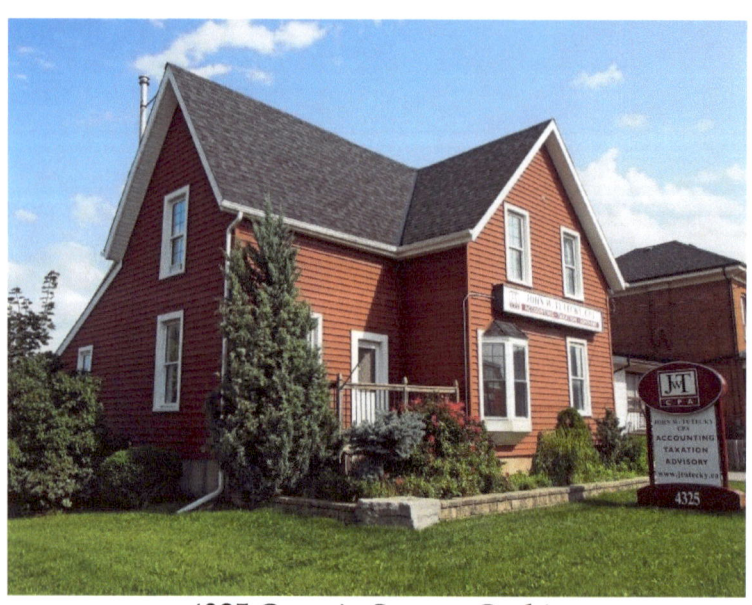

4325 Ontario Street - Gothic

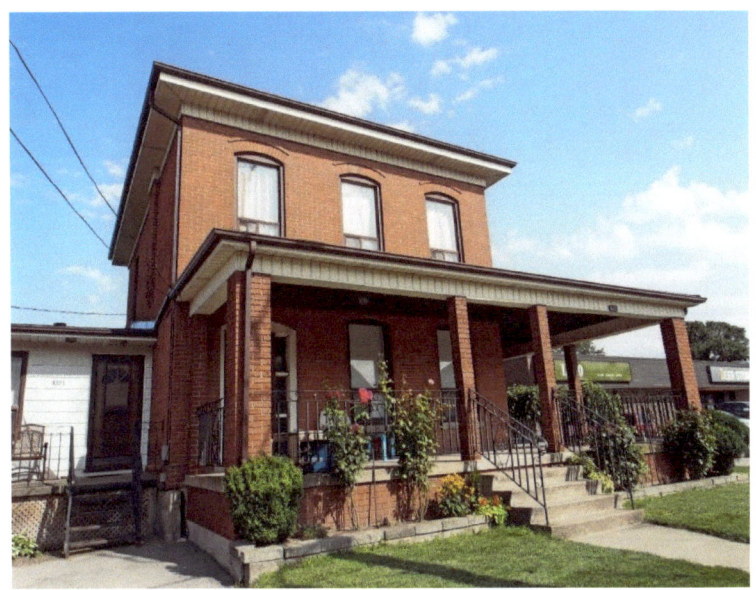

4321 Ontario Street

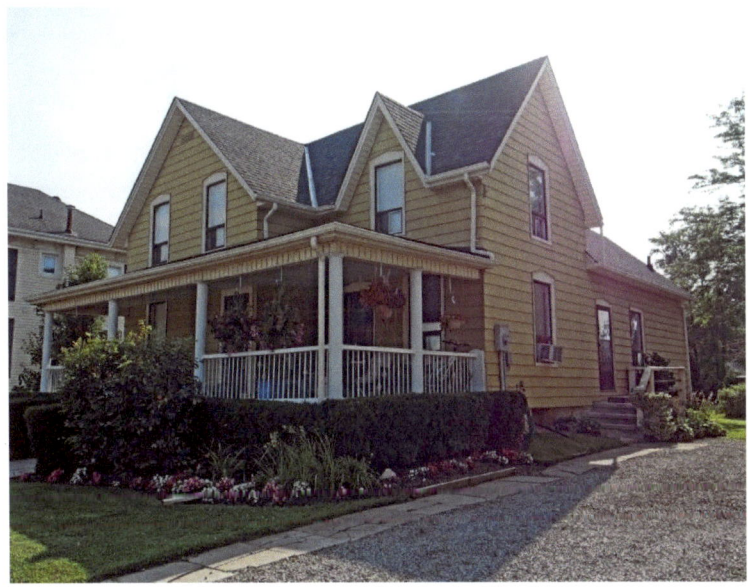

4318 Ontario Street - Gothic

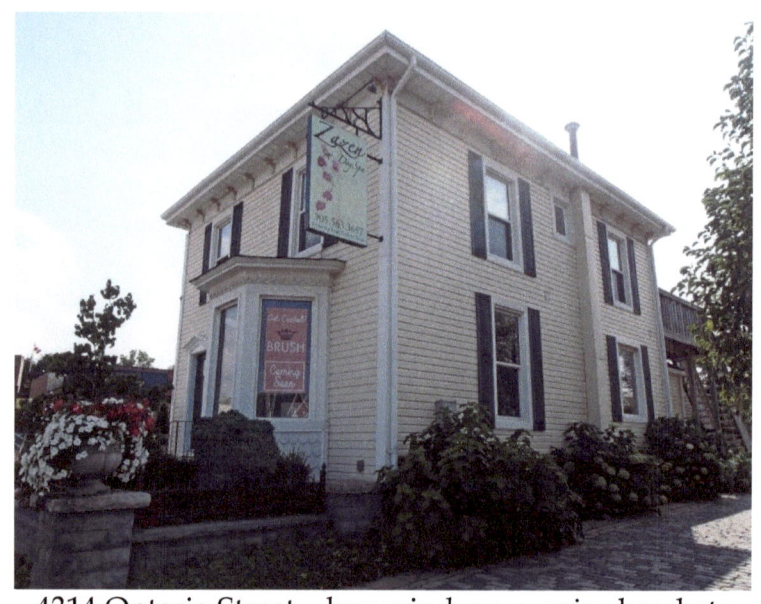

4314 Ontario Street – bay window, cornice brackets

Vineland

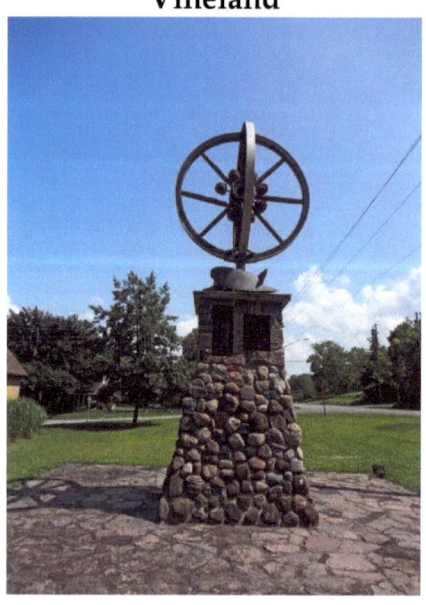

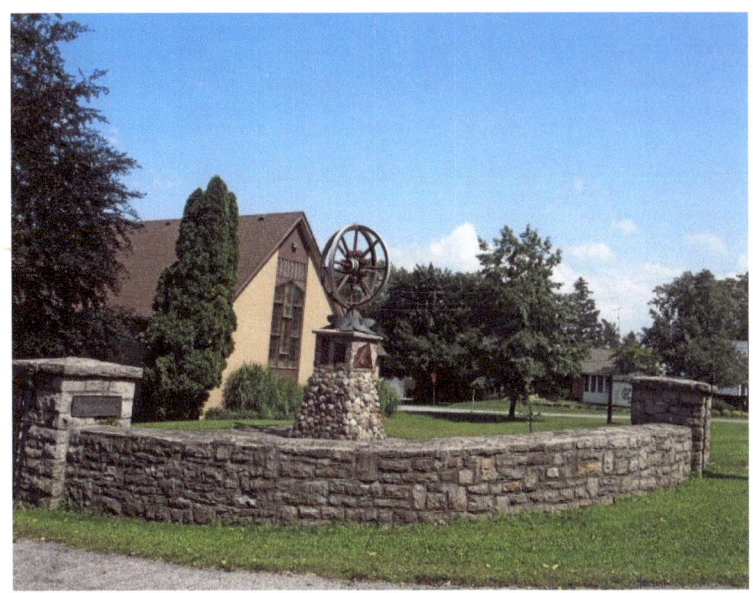

3557 Rittenhouse Road, Vineland

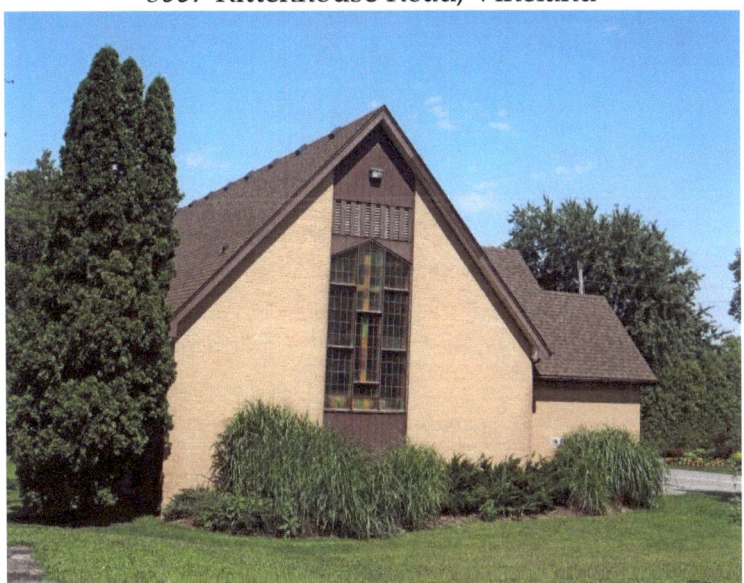

The First Mennonite Church in Vineland, adjacent to the cemetery at the corner of Regional Road 81 (former Highway 8) and Martin Road, organized in 1801, is the oldest Mennonite congregation in Canada. Mennonites were conscientious objectors to war and did not fight in the War of 1812.

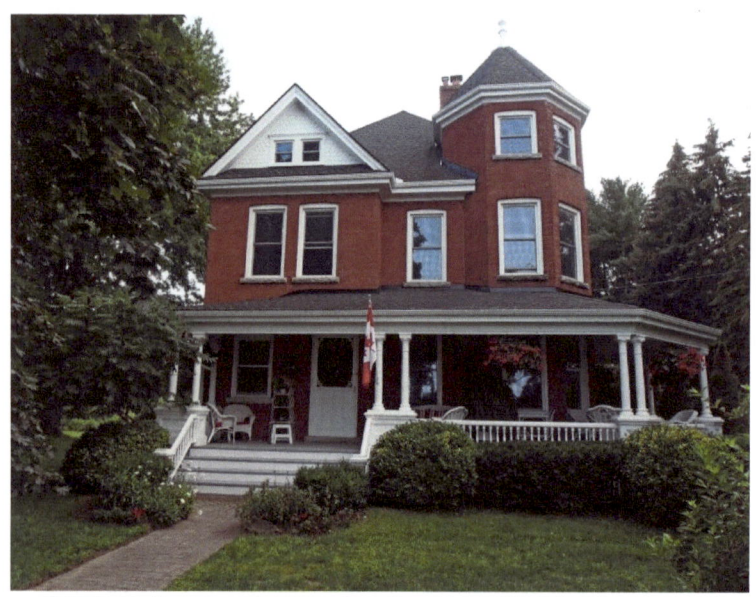

3150 Culp Road, Vineland – Overholdt House - The house was built in 1900 by a wealthy shipping merchant named Moses Overholdt. Built in red brick in the Queen Anne style, the house features a hipped room with diamond-shingled gables with Palladian windows on the sides, a three-storey hexagonal tower protruding from the northwest corner and topped with a finial, a wrap-around veranda with double piers on large bases, a tall corbeled chimney, and segmented, double-hung windows throughout.

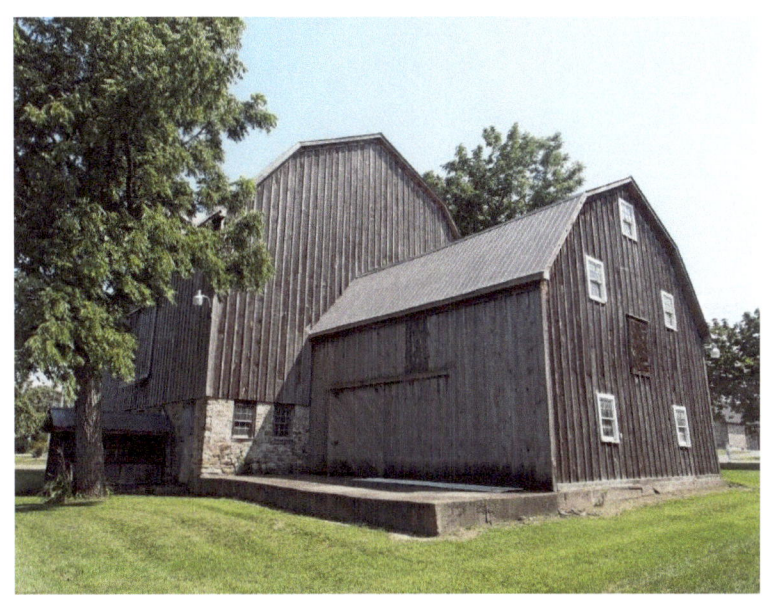

3227 Culp Road, Vineland – Kolb Culp Barn - 1851

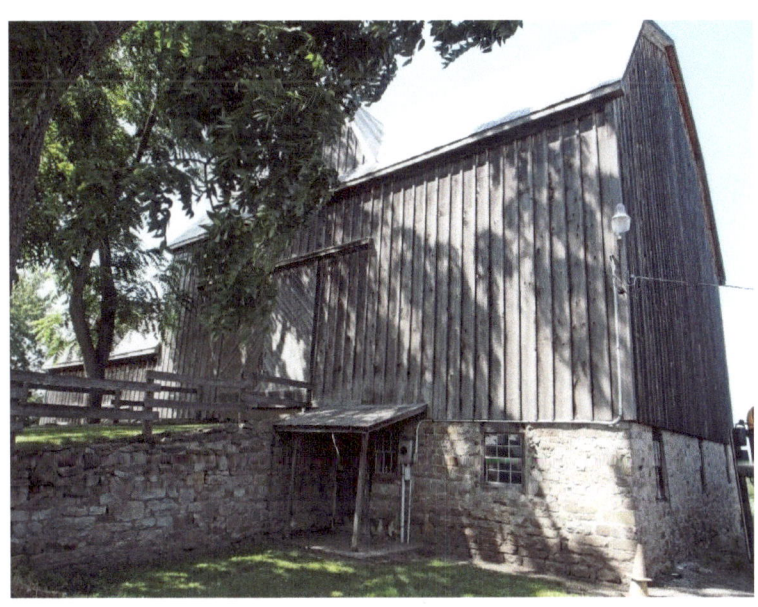

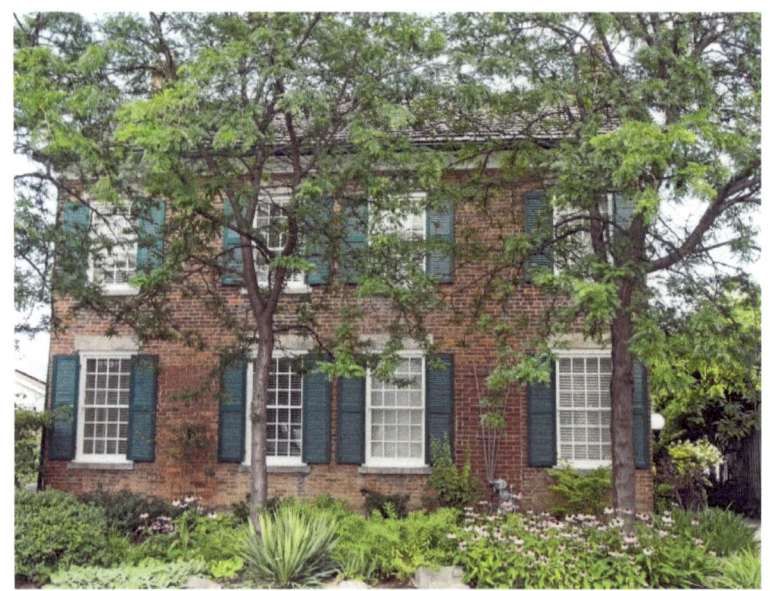

3853 Main Street, Jordan Station - Between 1840 and 1842 this Pennsylvania style house was built by local mason Newton Perry, for Isaac Wismer and his family. The red bricks were made in a kiln in the nearby Jordan Hollow.

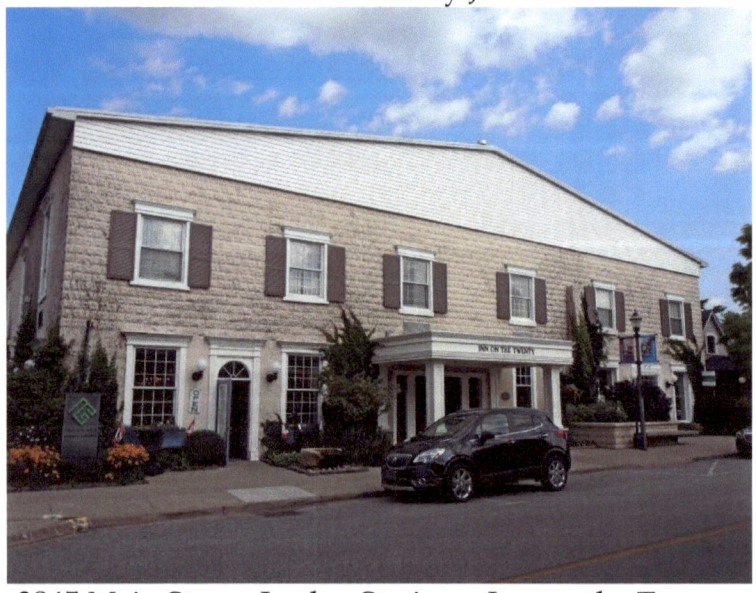

3845 Main Street, Jordan Station – Inn on the Twenty

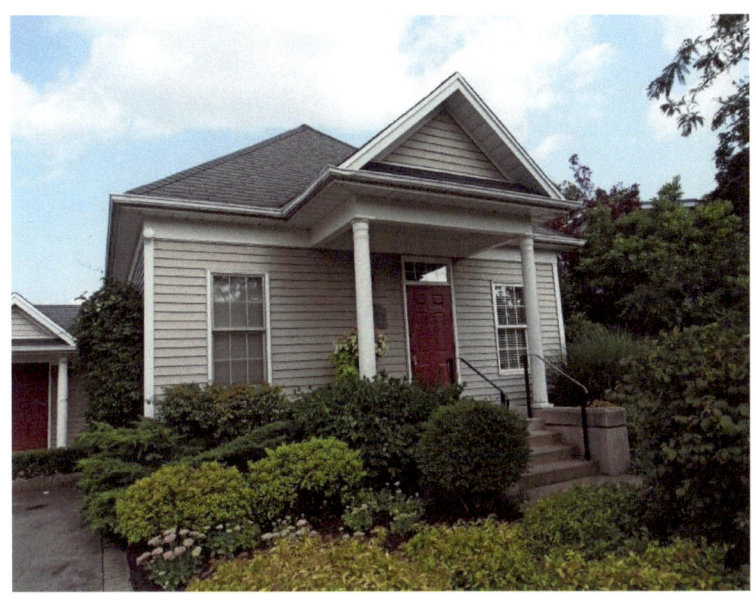

Main Street - Inn on the Twenty Winemaker's Cottage

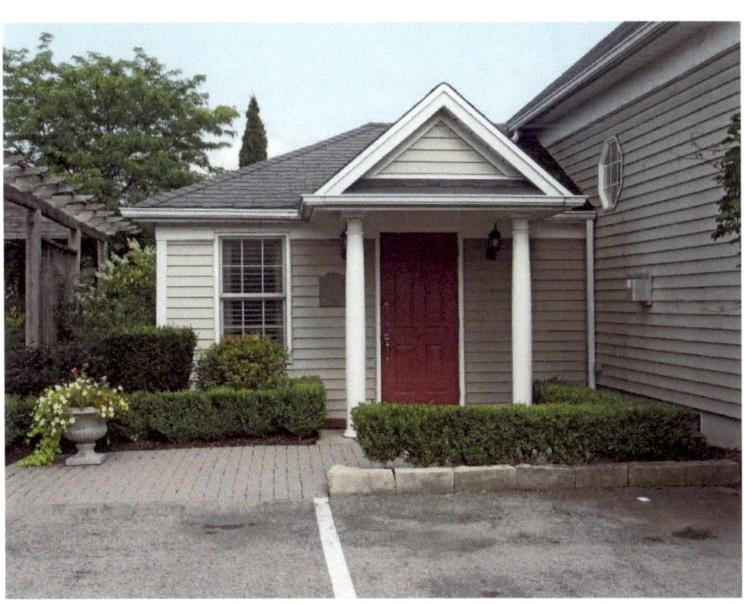

Inn on the Twenty Cooper's Cottage

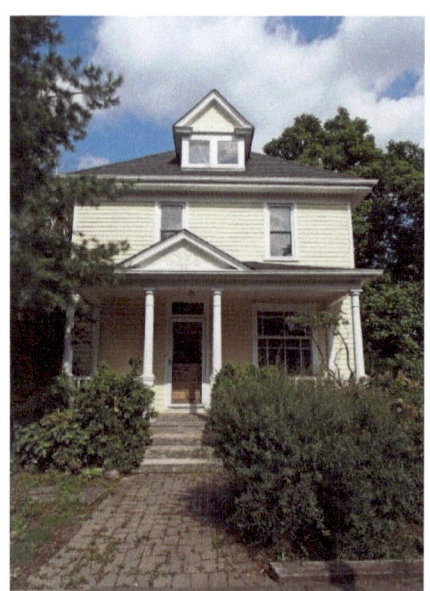
Main Street – dormer

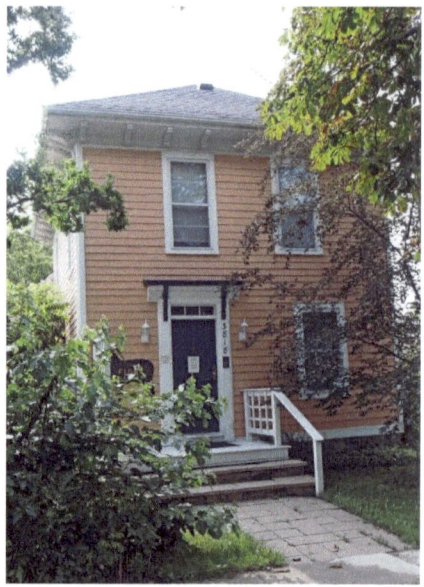
3818 Main Street

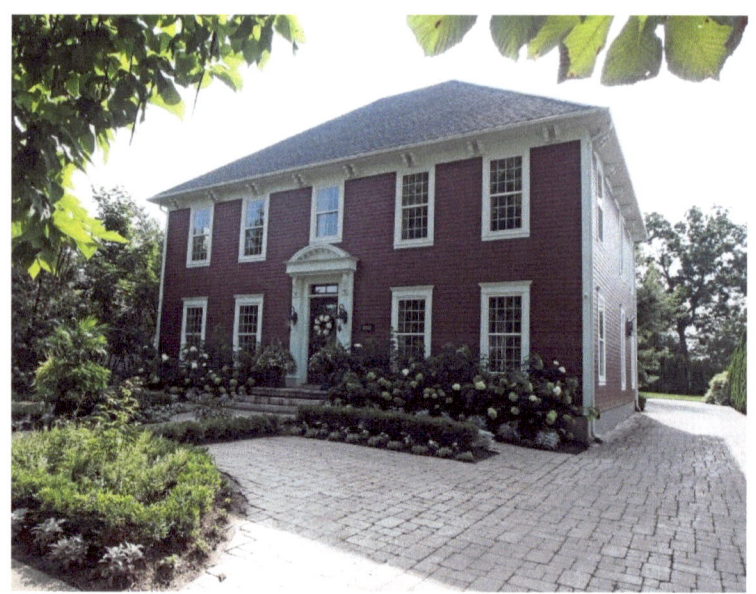
3812 Main Street, Jordan Station – Georgian style – curved pediment above door

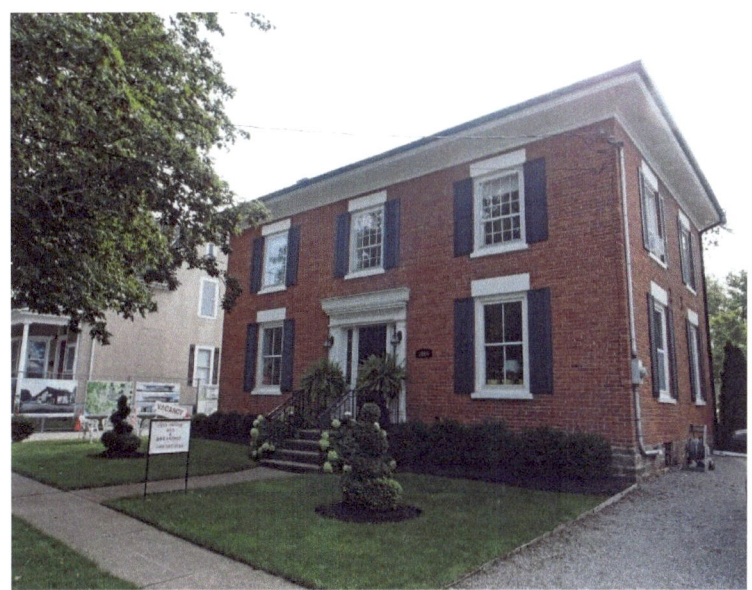

3804 Main Street, Jordan Station – The Honsberger-Griffith house was erected in 1851 by Michael Honsberger, a local merchant and Post Master in the Village of Jordan. The house was built in the Georgian style using local bricks.

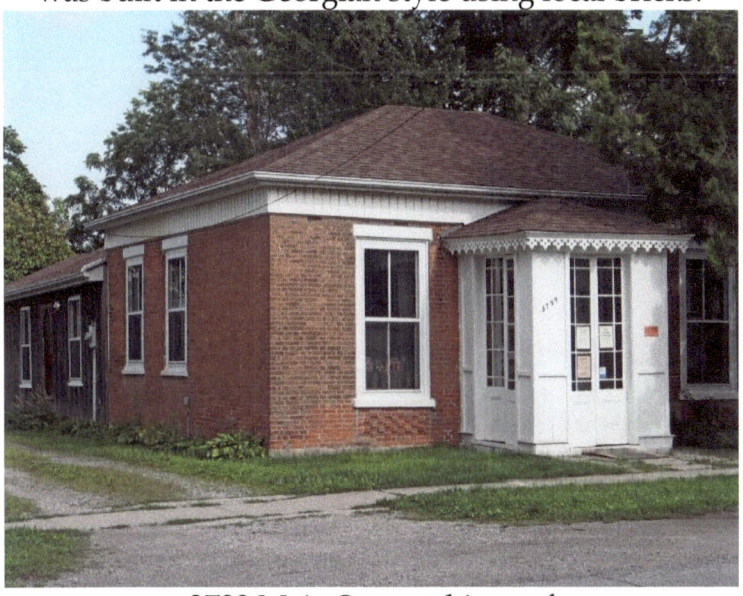

3799 Main Street – hip roof

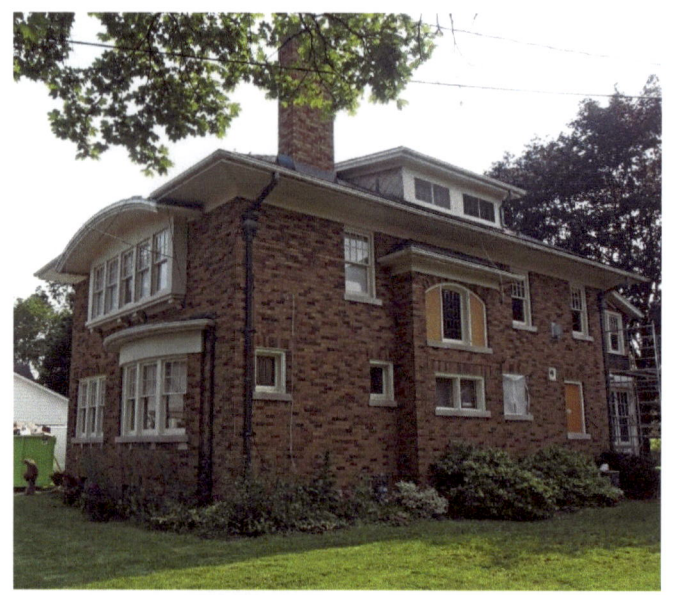

Main Street - dormer

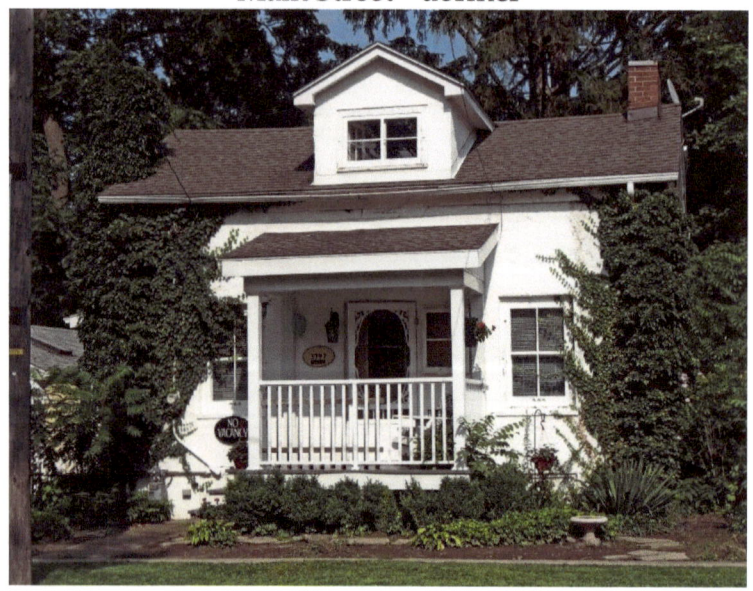

3797 Main Street – The Haynes-Griffin House is believed to have been built about 1829 by the Haynes family. It has an older above-ground cellar and had a weaving room dating from about 1812 - the Haynes family did weaving here.

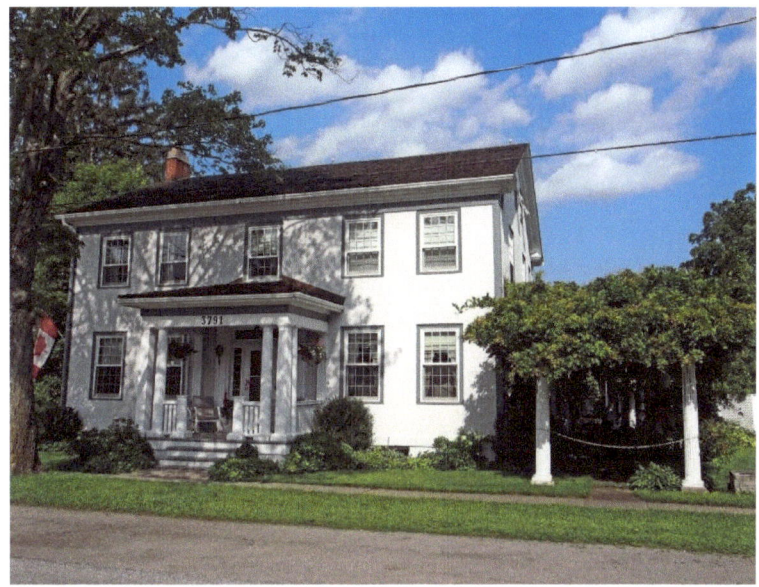

3791 Main Street – The Haynes-Creighton Georgian style home was built between 1844, when Isaac Overholt purchased the land, and 1855 when the house and land were sold to John Petty who was a carriage maker.

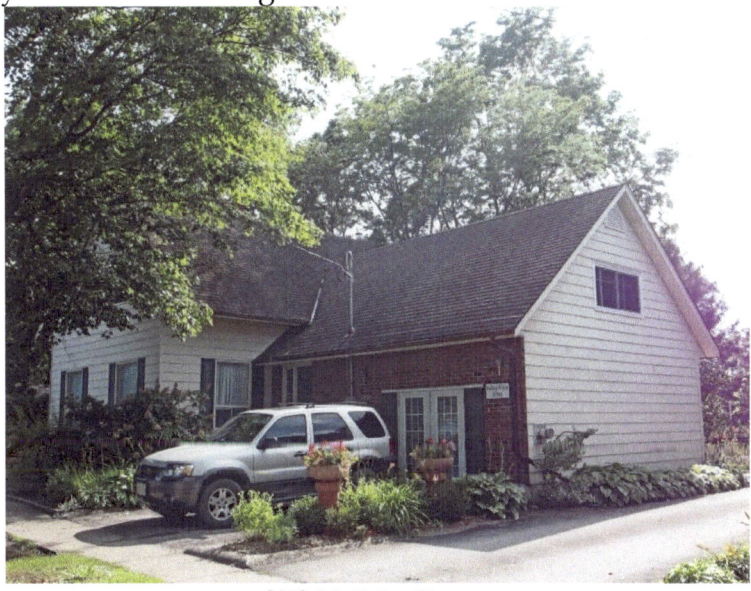

3784 Main Street

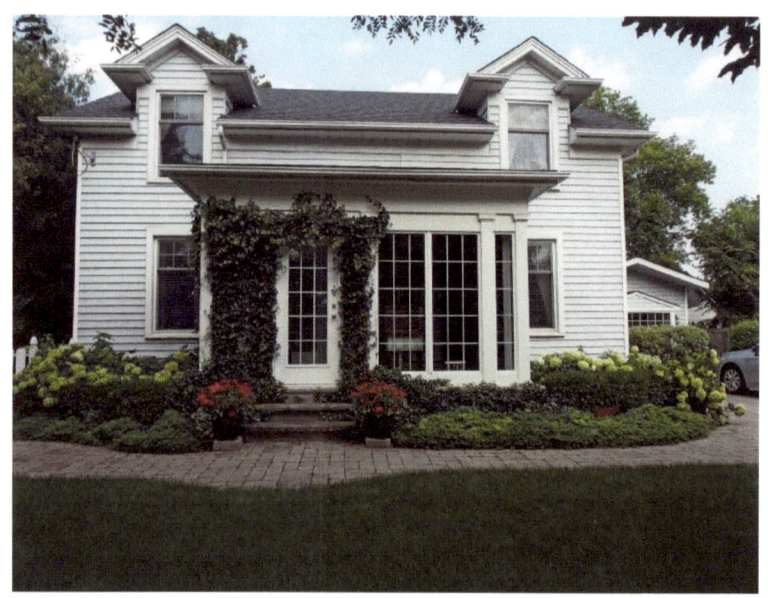

Main Street

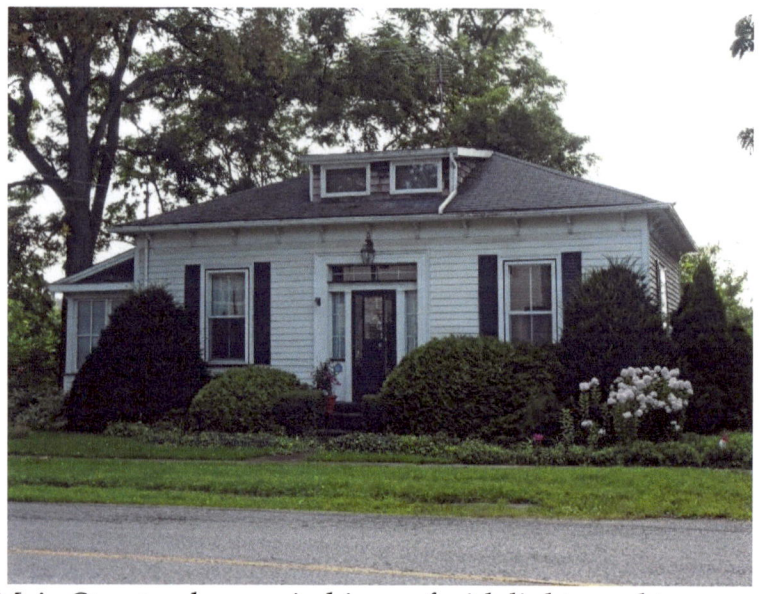

Main Street – dormer in hip roof, sidelights and transom

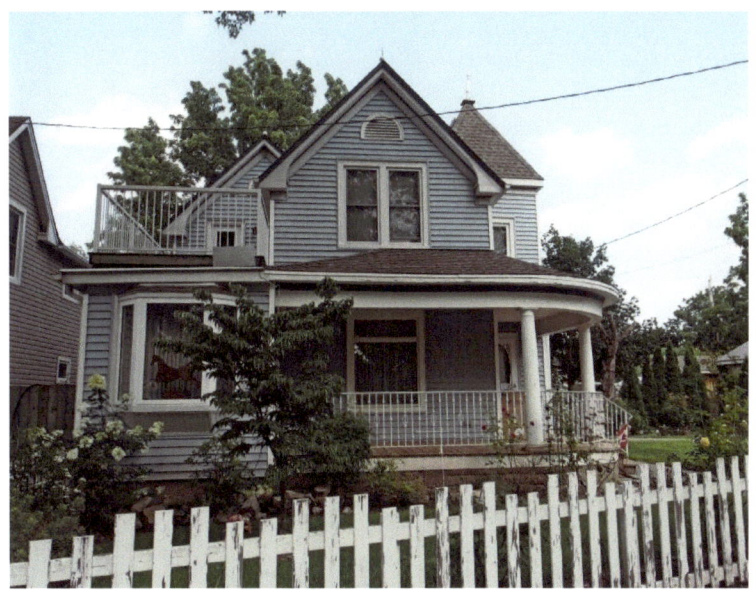

Main Street

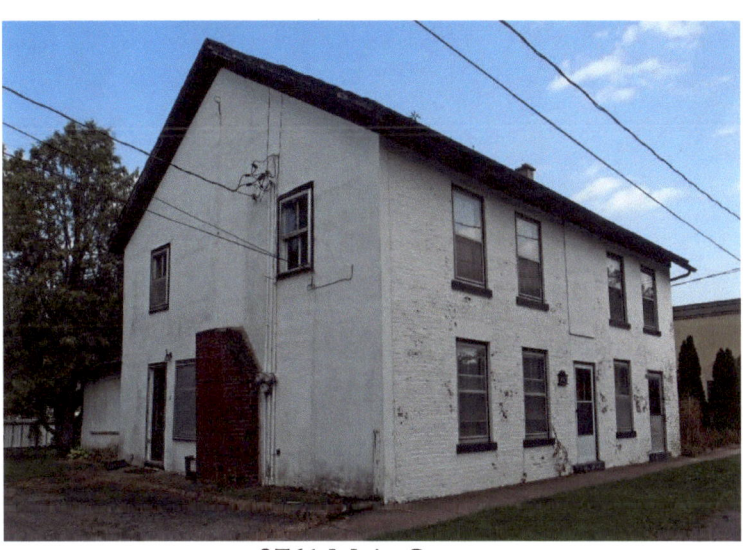

3761 Main Street

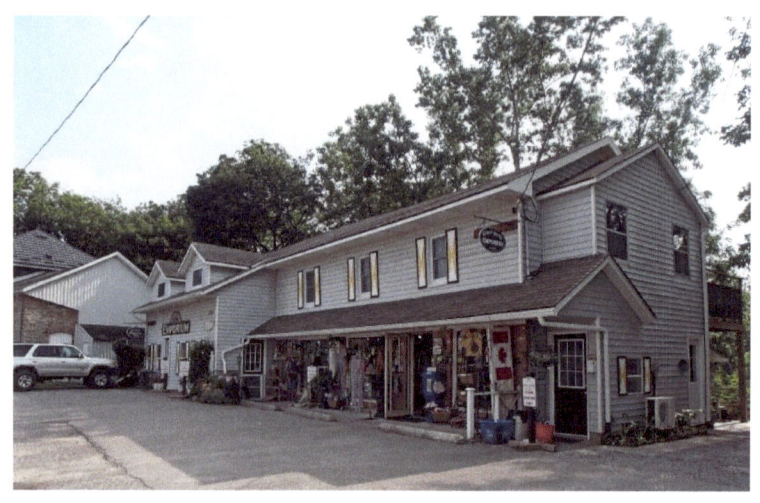

3744 Main Street

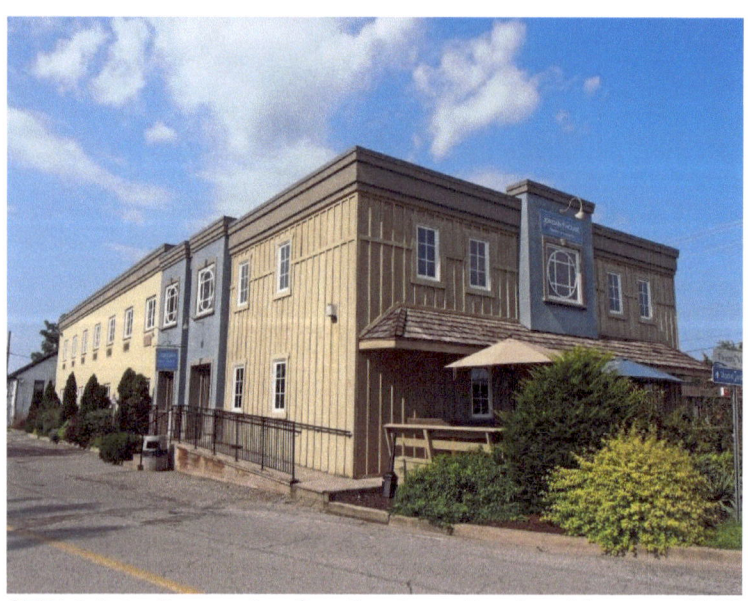

3751 Main Street, Jordan Station - Jordan House - 1842

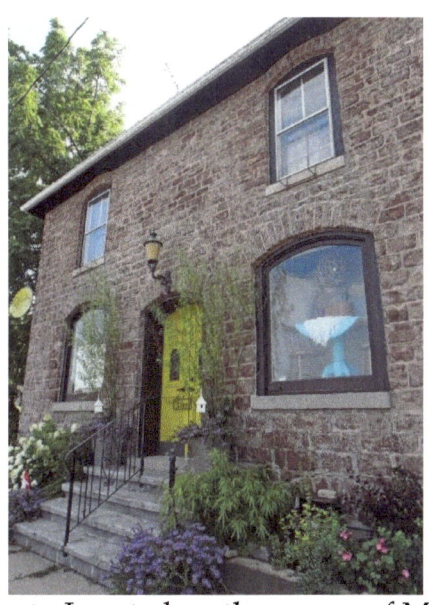

3738 Main Street - Located on the corner of Main Street and Regional Road 81/King Street, and built by James Snure, this house belonged to blacksmith and quarry owner Peter Zimmerman.

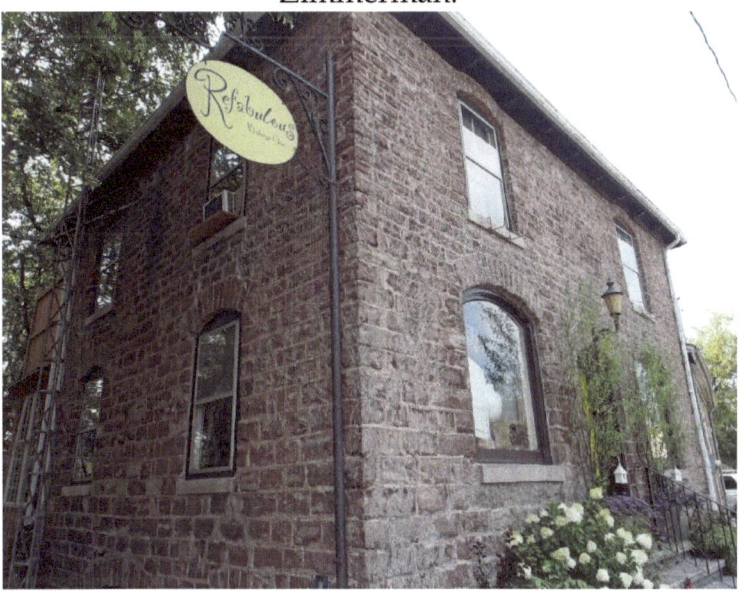

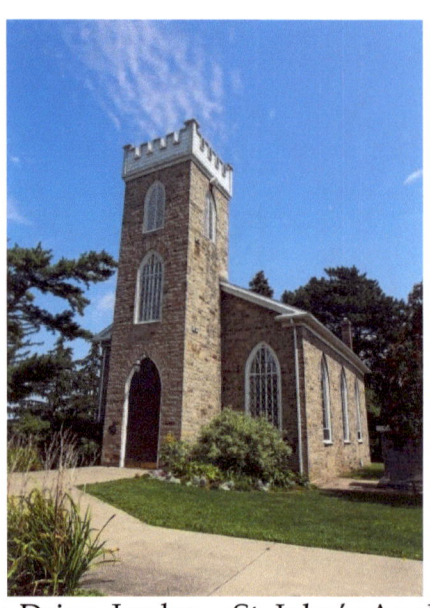

3685 McKenzie Drive, Jordan – St. John's Anglican Church – built in 1841 – three-storey tower with battlement, lancet windows

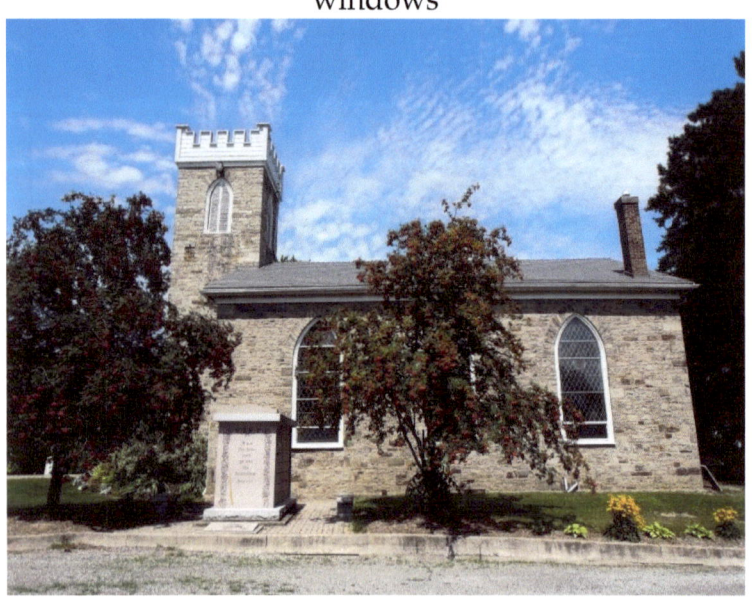

Ball's Falls

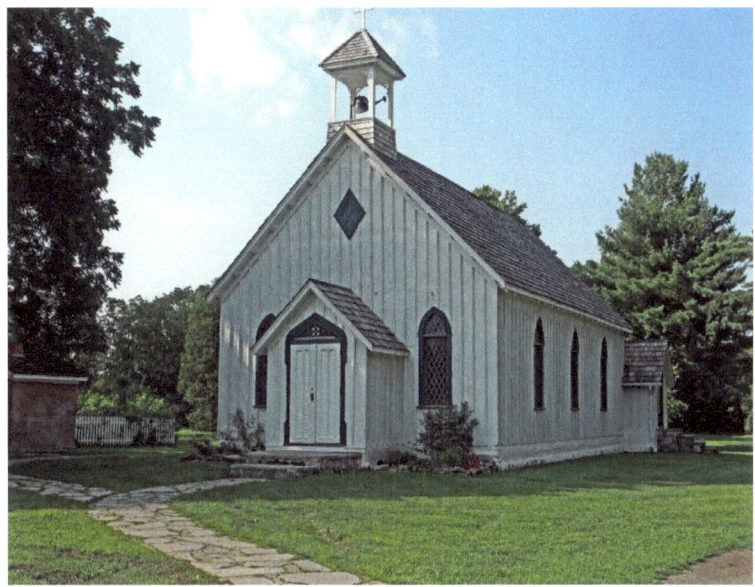

Historic Church at Ball's Falls

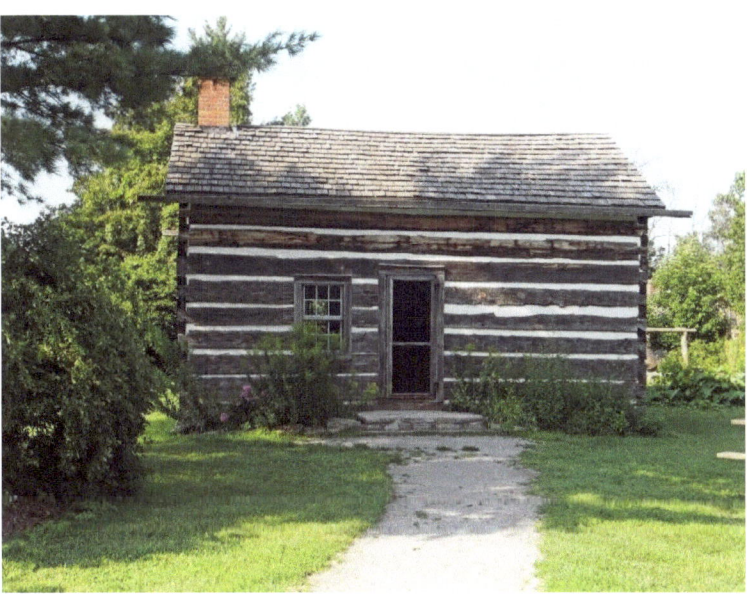

Log cabin

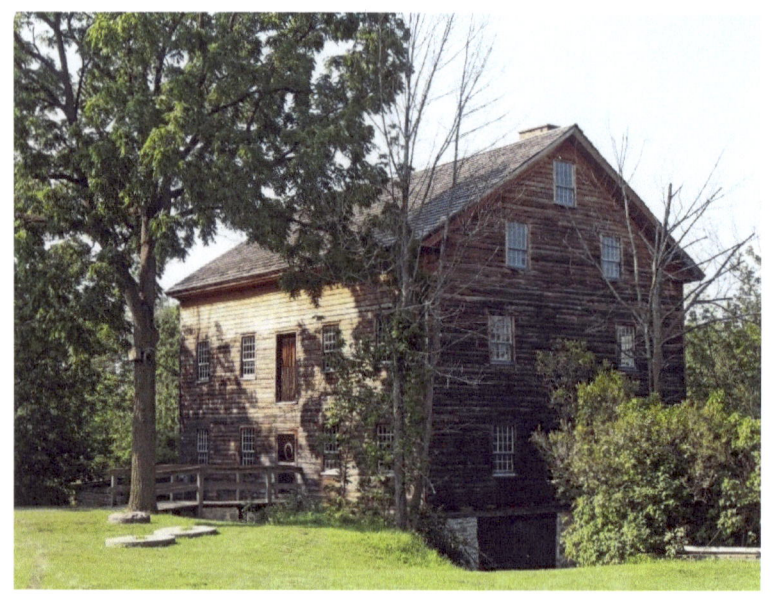

Ball's Falls Grist Mill

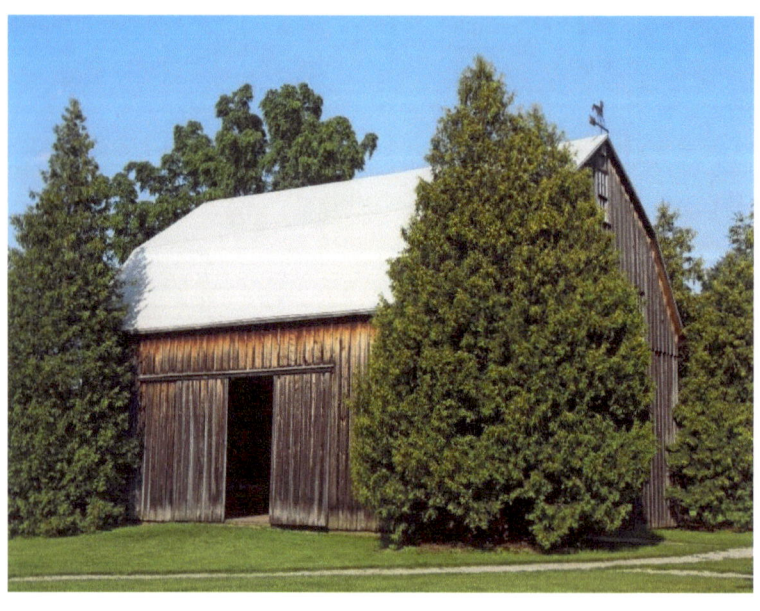

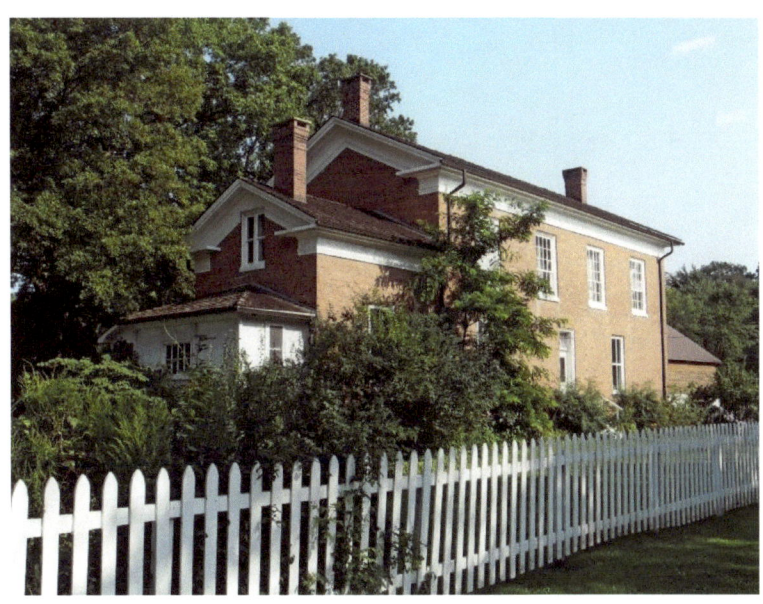

Ball Home

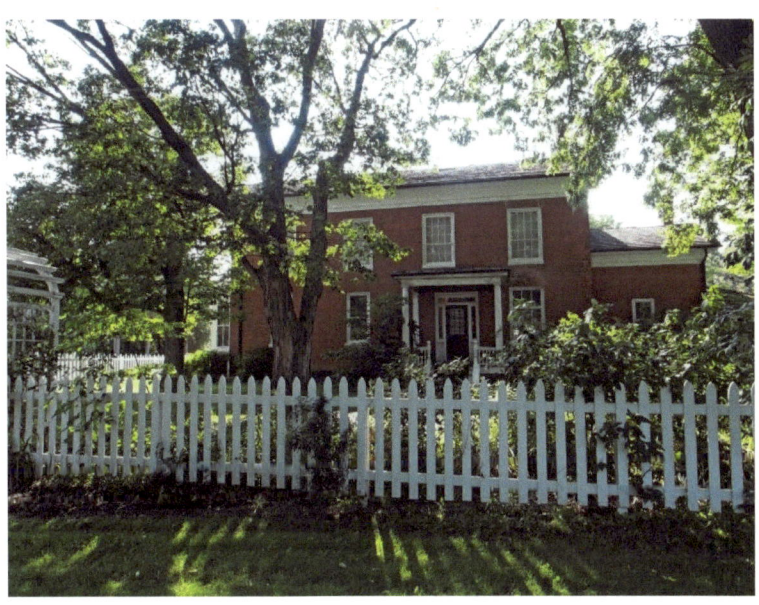

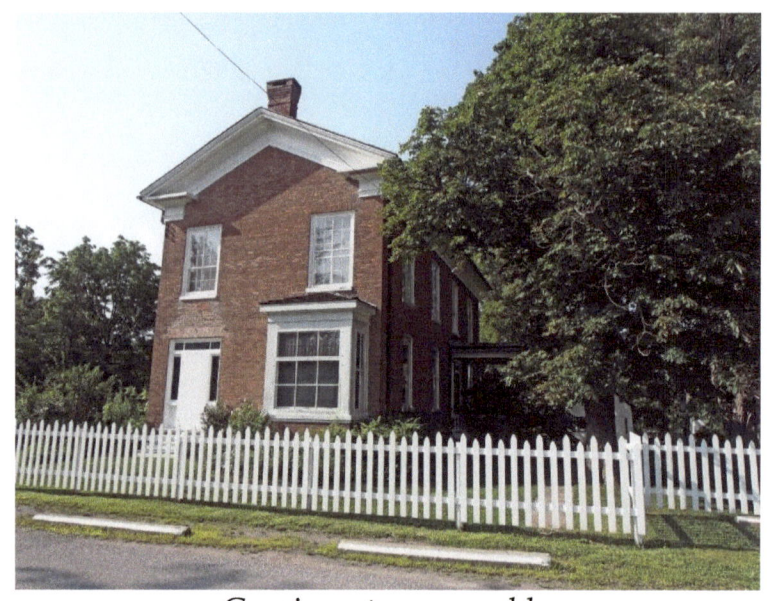
Cornice return on gable

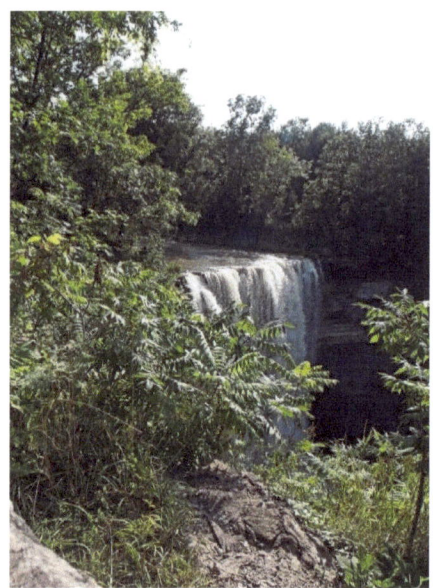
Ball's Fall

Campden

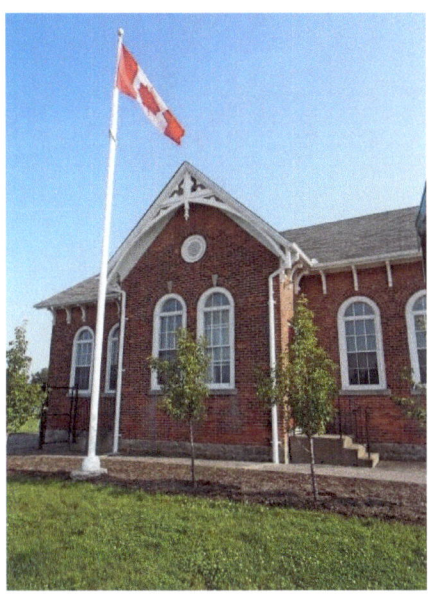

4160 Fly Road - Ebenezer Christian School, Campden – verge board trim on gable, voussoirs and keystones, cornice brackets

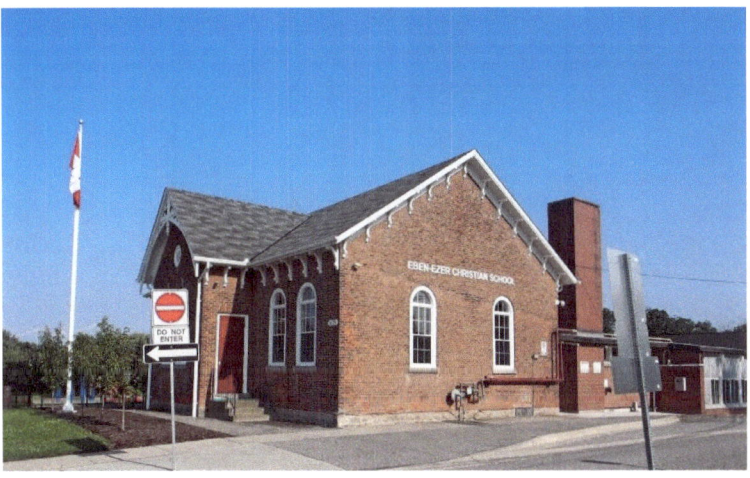

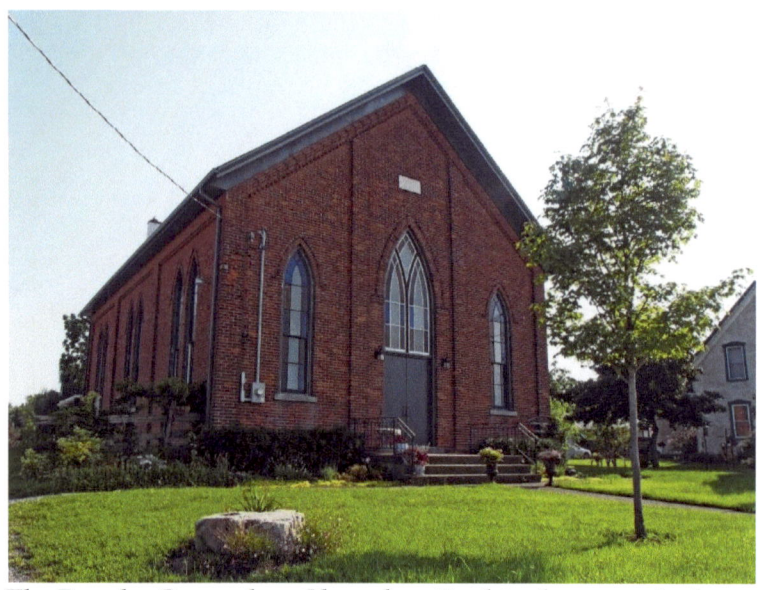

Fly Road - Campden Church – Gothic, lancet windows

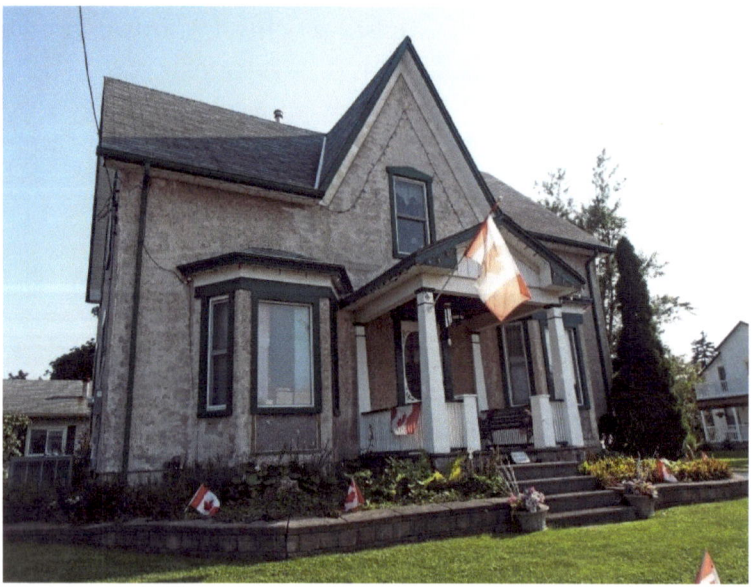

4176 Fly Road – Angel House – Gothic, bay windows

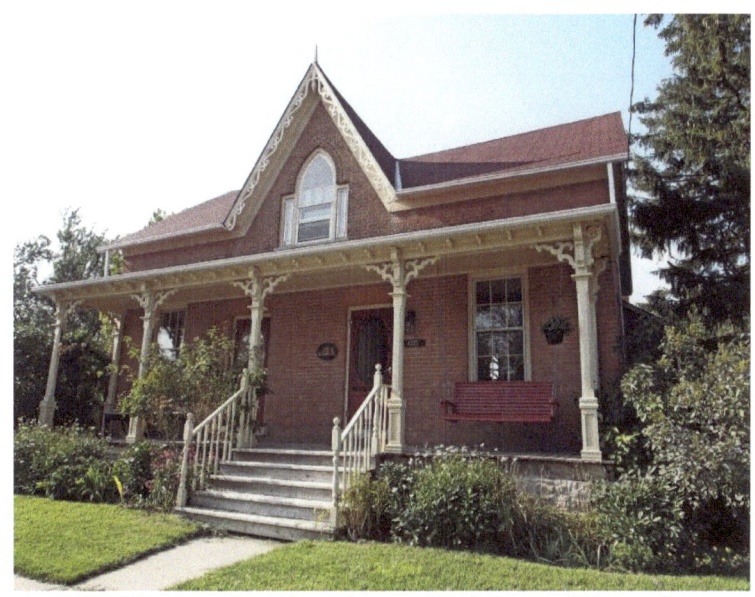

4225 Fly Road – The Henry W. Moyer-Humphrey House was built circa 1870 in the hamlet of Campden in the former Township of Clinton. This house is believed to be the first brick house in the hamlet; several members of the Moyer family have lived in the house. Henry W. Moyer was a tinsmith, auctioneer, insurance agent and the first postmaster. It is a classic 1½ storey farmhouse with Gothic ornamentation on the three gables and the full-width veranda. The front façade has two front doors and two windows with finished cut and tooled stone doorsteps and window sills. The steps are positioned to the right of centre. Each of the five square posts is decorated with spandrel brackets and decorative scrolls. The pitched roof has a front central gable with a carved finial. The center pointed arch window has sidelights supported by double header brick. The gable has decorative barge board. The windows are six-over-six panes.

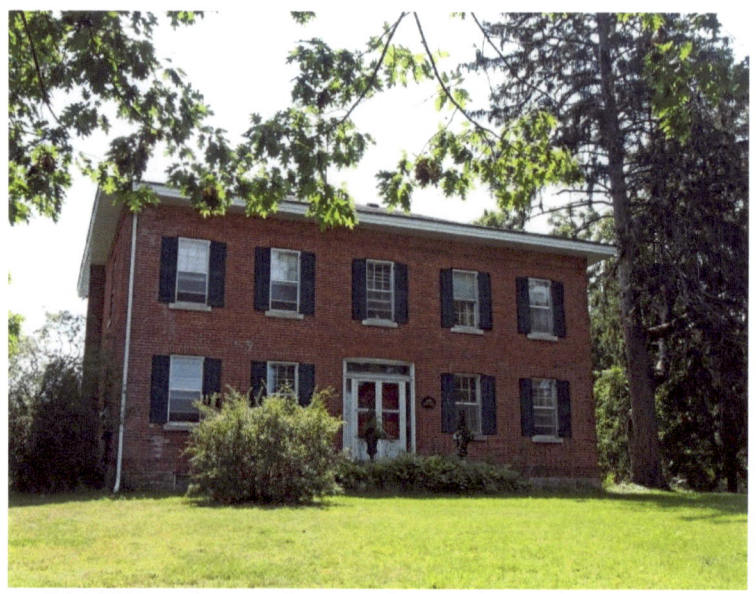

2044 King Street, Town of Lincoln – The house was built around 1860 by John David Crowe. The two-storey house is built of red brick in the late-Georgian style. The front façade is symmetrical with a double door surrounded by sidelights and an overhead transom. Surrounding the door are four lower and five upper windows, each double-hung, six-over-six with stone lintels at their base, segmented bricks on top and green shutters.

Architectural Terms

Battlement: A design for a parapet that has alternating solid parts and openings, originally used for defense, but later used as a decorative motif. Example: 3685 McKenzie Drive, Jordan, Page 56	
Bay Window: A window that projects out from a wall, in a semicircular, rectangular, or polygonal design. Used frequently in Gothic and Victorian designs. Example: 5545 King Street, Page 15	
Belvedere: (from the Italian "beautiful view") an architectural feature on a roof, in a garden or on a terrace that gives a beautiful view. Example: 4918 King Street, Page 18	
Brackets: a decorative or weight-bearing structural element which forms a right angle with one side against a wall and the other under a projecting surface such as an eave or roof. Example: 5545 King Street, Page 16	
Capital: The uppermost finish or decoration on a column. An Ionic column has a small base, a thin elegant shaft, and a capital composed of volutes which are carved whirls or twists that take the form of a scroll. A Doric column is characterized by a plain column with no base, a shaft with twenty flutings, and a simple capital with a simple entablature. Example: 4317 Central Avenue, Beamsville, Page 23	

Cornice Return: decorative element on the end of a gable. Example: 4287 William Street, Page 24	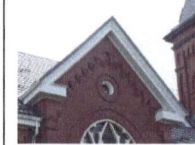
Cupola: A domed or curved roof rising from a building as a decorative element. Example: 4341 Ontario Street, Beamsville, Page 39	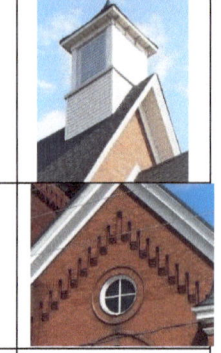
Dentil Moulding: an even series of rectangles used as ornamental decoration in cornices. Example: 4287 William Street, Page 24	
Dormer: (French for "sleep") a gable end window that pierces through the plane of a sloping roof surface to create usable space in the top floor or attic of a building by adding headroom. Example: 4915 King Street, Beamsville, Page 17	
Gable: the triangular portion of a wall between the edges of a sloping roof. **Jacobean Gable:** the gable extends above the roofline. Example: 5059 King Street, Beamsville, Page 11	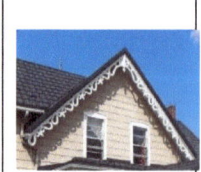
Hipped Roof: a roof where all sides slope downwards to the walls with no gables. Example: 5257 Philp Road, Page 34	
Keystones and Voussoirs: a voussoir is a wedge-shaped element used in building an arch. A keystone is the central stone that locks all the stones into position, allowing the arch to bear weight. Example: 4160 Fly Road, Campden, Page 61	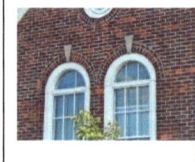

Lancet Window: a tall, narrow window with a pointed arch at its top. Example: 3685 McKenzie Drive, Jordan, Page 56	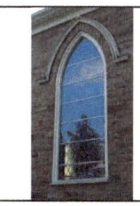
Muntin: When a window unit has more than one pane, the material that separates the panes is called the muntin. The larger, more decorative separations are called mullions. In stained glass windows, each piece of colored glass is held in place by a muntin. These were traditionally made of iron. Example: 4287 William Street, Page 24	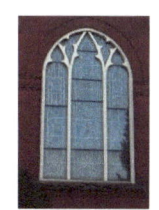
Pediment: a triangular section above the door or portico, usually supported by columns. The inside of the triangle is called the tympanum. Example: 4260 Queen Street, Beamsville, Pg. 27	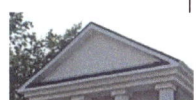
Sidelight: a vertical window that flanks a door, and is often used to emphasize the importance of a primary entrance. **Transom Window:** the light above the doorway, also called a fanlight. Example: 2044 King Street, Page 64	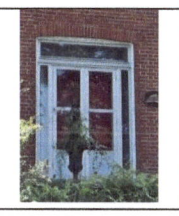
Tower: A circular, square, or octagonal vertical structure higher than the surrounding structure that is usually part of an existing building and is created either for extra defense or for a specific purpose such as a clock or a bell tower. Example: 3685 McKenzie Drive, Jordan, Page 56	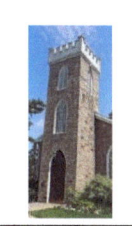
Verge board and Finial: also called bargeboards – hang from the projecting end of a roof and are often elaborately carved and ornamented. **Finial:** ornament added to the top of a gable, pinnacle, canopy or spire. Example: 5074 King Street, Page 11	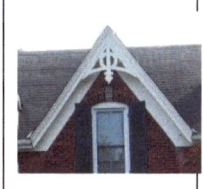

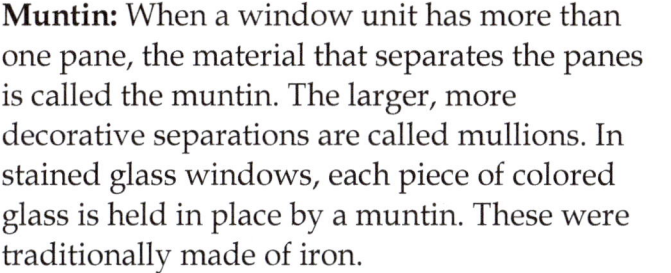

Building Styles

Georgian, before 1860 – This style began with the British King Georges in the 18th century. These buildings have balanced facades around a central door, medium-pitched gable roofs, and small paned windows. Example: 3812 Main St., Jordan Station, Pg.48	
Gothic Revival, 1830-1890 – These decorative buildings have sharply-pitched gables with highly detailed verge boards, pointed-arch window openings, and dichromatic brickwork. It is a common style in Ontario. Example: 5053 King Street, Beamsville, Pg. 9	
Queen Anne, 1885-1900 – This style is distinguished by an irregular outline featuring a combination of an offset tower, broad gables, projecting two-storey bays, verandahs, multi-sloped roofs, and tall, decorative chimneys. A mixture of brick and wood is common. Windows often have one large single-paned bottom sash and small panes in the upper sash. Example: 5600 King Street West, Page 5	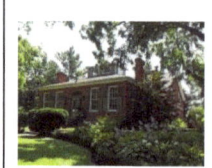
Regency Cottage, 1830-1860 – This style originated in England in 1815 and spread to Ontario later in the 19th century as British officers retired to Canada. It is a modest one-storey house with a low-pitched hip roof and has a symmetrical front façade. Example: 4918 King Street, Beamsville, Page 18	

www.ingramcontent.com/pod-product-compliance
Lightning Source LLC
Chambersburg PA
CBHW040231220526
45473CB00001B/198